SMALL HOMES

579

DESIGN
IDEAS FOR GREAT AMERICAN HOUSES

SMALL HOMES

From the Editors of **Fine Homebuilding**

The Taunton Press

The Taunton Press, Inc., 63 South Main Street, PO Box 5506, Newtown, CT 06470-5506
e-mail: tp@taunton.com

Distributed by Publishers Group West

JACKET AND COVER DESIGN: Ann Marie Manca
INTERIOR DESIGN: Cathy Cassidy
LAYOUT: Cathy Cassidy
COVER PHOTOGRAPHERS: Front cover: David Ericson. Back cover: Andy Engle, courtesy
Fine Homebuilding, © The Taunton Press, Inc. (left); Tom O'Brien (top right); Charles
Bickford, courtesy *Fine Homebuilding,* © The Taunton Press, Inc. (center); David
Ericson, courtesy *Fine Homebuilding,* © The Taunton Press, Inc. (bottom right).

LIBRARY OF CONGRESS CATALOGING-IN-PUBLICATION DATA:

Small homes : design ideas for great American houses.
      p. cm.
"From the editors of Fine homebuilding."
  ISBN 1-56158-654-4
  1. Small houses. I. Fine homebuilding.

TH4890 .S63 2002
690'.8--dc21

                                    2002154946

Printed in the United States of America
10 9 8 7 6 5 4 3 2 1

Contents

Introduction

In the late 1940s, William Levitt started buying up potato fields on Long Island, New York, and building houses. To meet the needs of servicemen returning home from World War II, he built one-story, two-bedroom Capes that measured less than 800 sq. ft. Fifty years later, the average new home in this country is three times that size, and it gets bigger every year. I'm not sure why we want bigger and bigger houses (unless it's to store all of our unused exercise equipment), but I wish it weren't the case.

Smaller houses require fewer resources to build. They're less expensive to heat, cool, and maintain. And generally speaking, I'd rather see money spent on great details than on drywall acreage. The tide may yet turn. That first wave of baby boomers, many of whom were born in Levittown, are approaching 60 now. And they're starting to think about smaller, one-story houses that would be easier to clean and to get around in.

With the hope of encouraging smaller homes, we've collected 22 articles from past issues of *Fine Homebuilding* that feature houses under 2,400 sq. ft. (anything smaller than the national average qualifies as small in our book). Written by builders and architects from all over the country, these articles cover a diversity of styles, materials, locations, and programs. But each of them explores one central issue: how do you make the most of a small space?

—*Kevin Ireton*, editor-in-chief

When Builder Weds Architect

FOLKS MUST HAVE THOUGHT THAT SUSAN AND I WERE A little crazy when we set our wedding date to fall about a third of the way through the construction of our house. But I have a lot of confidence in myself as a builder and in my wife as an architect. So I figured that building our own home would be stress-free.

Not hardly. A client's choices are typically limited in part by a builder's guidance. But we had no such limitations. Susan opted to keep track of design ideas by collecting them in a loose-leaf binder, and she'd filled three binders before we were done. I filled my own folder with systems information, and as choices mounted, decisions for my own place seemed to come more slowly than those I make for clients. In the end, we made our choices by juggling cost, function, availability, quality, and, of course, a number of aesthetic variables.

A Wet, Sloping Lot Dictates Design

About all I can draw is a square cut on a 2x4, so when we came to the design of the house, I gladly looked on as Susan did her first sketches in the time-honored tradition: on restaurant napkins. The land we selected helped to drive the design process. The grade sloped away from the street, so we decided to put the garage under the house in the back where it would be hidden (see photo p. 6). But because the rear of the lot was wet and densely forested, the area between the house and the street was the only space for the yard, a challenge we'd tackle later.

Susan's wish list of design features included a light, bright, open interior with tall ceilings, lots of built-in storage space, an exterior that fit in with the neighborhood, and a garden area. Because I was building this house

Private fenced-in patio becomes a three-season room. A fence around the brick patio provides privacy for the master bedroom but also forms a large outdoor room for informal entertaining. Photo taken at A on floor plan.

Hiding the garage from the street. A sloping lot created the perfect place to tuck the garage under the back of the house, where it can't be seen from the street. Meanders in the driveway provide ample parking for guests. Photo taken at E on floor plan. Photo by Roe A. Osborn

We made our choices by juggling cost, function, availability, quality, and of course a number of aesthetic variables.

mostly without extra help, I wanted to simplify construction details as much as possible. For example, I used lightweight I-joists for all the floor framing. Another goal was to build the house as tight as possible and to use energy-efficient low-e argon-filled glass in all the windows and doors. These features—along with orienting the house properly for solar gain—would make it practical in its energy consumption. We decided that we could fit all our needs into a Cape-style home, and by the fourth sketch, Susan had a workable design.

We took our sketches and notes to an architect friend of Susan's, Nancy Santagata, bartering a day's worth of tree-trimming in exchange for the final CAD plans. Nancy suggested raising the exterior walls 3 ft. above the floor to create more headroom in the narrow second-floor bedroom. She also recommended 18-in. eaves, a bit wider than traditional eaves in these parts. Wider overhangs would shield the south-facing glass doors in front of the house from the summer sun and offer some shelter for the entry off the front deck.

Tall Ceilings in the Great Room

The house consists of two perpendicular sections: One is 22 ft. by 28 ft. with its ridge roughly parallel to the street, and the other section is 16 ft. by 30 ft. (see floor plans p. 8).

The basement level houses the garage, the workshop, and the utilities. The main floor includes the living room, dining room,

LEFT Raised ceiling opens great room. The kitchen, living room, and dining room share one open area from the front to the back of the house. At 9 ft. tall, the ceilings permit awning windows over French doors. Photo taken at C on floor plan.

ABOVE No alarm clock needed. With the head of the bed in this south-facing bump-out, sleeping past sunrise is out of the question. Photo taken at F on floor plan.

LEFT Built-in bed in a bump-out. The bed for the master bedroom is built into a bay window. The fenced-in patio provides the privacy. Photo taken at G on floor plan.

A SIMPLE HOUSE THAT PUTS A PREMIUM ON SPACE

Within the confines of an uncomplicated Cape, the author and his wife figured out how to make good use of every square inch of space. Aside from turning every nook and cranny into usable storage, they put pocket doors on the first-floor bath to let it be used both as a visitors' bathroom and as part of the master bath. A large fenced-in brick patio in front of the house functions as a three-season room.

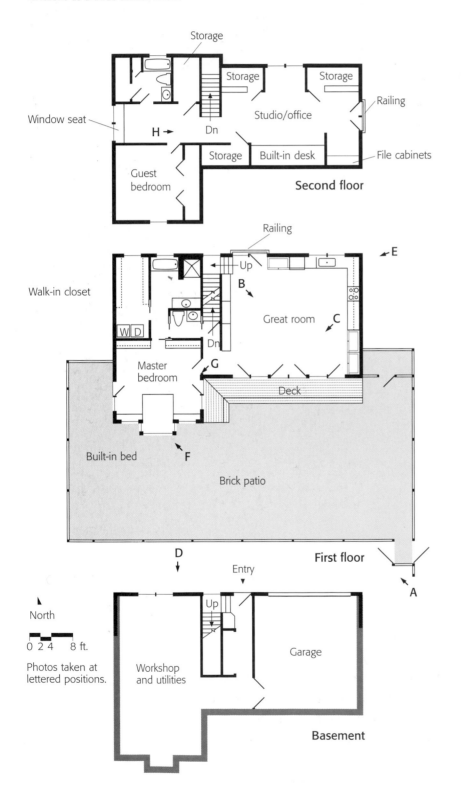

Storage

Storage

Storage

Railing

Window seat

H →

Dn

Studio/office

Built-in desk

File cabinets

Storage

Guest bedroom

Second floor

Railing

E

Up

B

Walk-in closet

Great room

C

W D

Dn

G

Master bedroom

Deck

Built-in bed

F

Brick patio

D

Entry

First floor

A

North

0 2 4   8 ft.

Photos taken at lettered positions.

Up

Workshop and utilities

Garage

Basement

SPECS

BEDROOMS: **2**

BATHROOMS: **2**

SIZE: **1,950 sq. ft. (heated space)**

COST: **$68.00 per sq. ft.**

COMPLETED: **1998**

LOCATION: **East Greenwich, Rhode Island**

ARCHITECTS: **Susan Aitcheson & Nancy Santagata**

BUILDER: **Mike Guertin**

Jam-packed but comfortable office. Doors on both sides of the second-floor office provide access to storage in spaces that most houses rarely use. Shed dormers provide headroom above a built-in desk and a drafting table. Photo taken at H on floor plan.

and kitchen in one large room. Dividing the space into three separate rooms would have given each of the rooms a claustrophobic feeling; leaving the room open meshed with our informal lifestyle and manner of entertaining. Susan thought that ceilings at least 9 ft. high were necessary to give such a large room proper scale (see photo top p. 7).

Our master-bedroom suite completes the first floor. When we decided to build our bed into a bump-out that faced the street (see photos bottom and right p. 7) the

privacy fence planned for a year or so down the line took on greater urgency. In addition to hiding the bedroom from the street, the cedar fence encloses a 1,500-sq.-ft. recycled-brick patio that acts as our three-season room (see photo p. 4).

Numerous flower beds inside the fence give us bright blossoms from early spring to late autumn. Because most guests tend to use the fence gate as the front door to the house, I wired the doorbell to a button on the fence post beside the gate.

The top floor is an open study and office space that continues the entire length of the house (see photo p. 9). In the adjoining section opposite the office area is a guest bedroom with a sitting area and bath.

Custom Cabinets and Recycled Materials Cut Costs

Custom cabinets are usually expensive and complicated, but I kept the cabinetry in the kitchen and living room simple (see photo below). To save on materials, I used the walls as the backs of the cabinets. I made the upper cabinets a nonstandard 44 in. tall with a 3-in. bottom rail to conceal full-size fluorescent fixtures beneath the cabinets. Crown molding along the top of the cabinets hides other fluorescent fixtures that bounce light off the ceiling for simple and effective full-room illumination. Because I was not set up for making cabinet doors, I left that task to an expert at a local cabinet shop.

We used a combination of new and old materials in building the house. The floors were framed with I-joists because of their ability to span greater lengths than dimensional lumber. But when we needed long 2x6 studs to balloon-frame the exterior walls, we recycled rafters from a roof I tore off a small ranch house. The 2x6s were knot-free, rock-hard, dry Douglas fir.

Susan chose reclaimed chestnut for the floors on the main floor, and our kitchen cabinets are made of reclaimed hemlock. The chestnut ate up our flooring budget, so for the upstairs floor, I lightly sanded and used polyurethane on the oriented strand board subfloor. It was a quick, inexpensive solution, and we can add finished flooring on top whenever we choose.

Exterior Materials That Balance Aesthetics and Low Maintenance

Susan and I had to compromise on the exterior finish. If I had my way, the house would have been sided with vinyl to keep maintenance down. But Susan insisted on white-cedar shingles, a more aesthetically correct siding material. The shingles will require only an occasional coat of transparent stain to extend their life after they start

Custom cabinets of recycled hemlock. The author custom-built all the cabinetry in the house without making complicated carcases that take a lot of time and material. Photo taken at B on floor plan.

to turn a little gray. I wove two geese into the shingles on the back of the house (see photo right). They came out so nicely that I wish I'd had the courage to put them on the front.

The trim was another matter. I wanted to wrap all of it with white aluminum, but Susan wasn't keen on that idea. We agreed to wrap all the high rake boards, and Susan painted all the window trim and cornerboards. Fascias would be covered by gutters, so it made no sense to waste perfectly good redwood beneath them. Instead, I wrapped the 2x6 subfascias with aluminum. Susan let me finish the higher soffits with vented vinyl, but she insisted on painted AC plywood for the lower, more-visible soffits in front. I also chose rot-resistant ipé for the deck; it will never need refinishing.

Wall goose. A red-cedar goose woven into the white-cedar shingles adds a decorative touch to the backside of the house. Photo taken at D on floor plan.

A House That's Easy on the Wallet

Energy efficiency was one of my biggest concerns when designing and building this house. Besides choosing energy-efficient windows and meticulously creating a tight building envelope, I eliminated all window headers and trimmers in walls that had nothing bearing from above and used an exterior-corner detail, which allows continuous insulation around the corner. Less wood makes these details simpler to build and minimizes conductive-heat loss through the wood in the walls. I also airsealed the plate-to-subfloor connections as well as all floor-to-floor penetrations and areas around windows and doors with low-expansion foam.

Capes can be difficult to insulate and air-seal, so I set the rafters on top of the finished second-floor deck rather than using the traditional method of setting the rafters on top of the wall plates next to the floor joists. After custom-fitting foil-faced foam

vent chutes to the underside of the roof sheathing, I sheathed the bottoms of the rafters with 6-mil poly held in place with 1x3 strapping. Then I stapled reinforced poly to the exterior-wall studs and had the rafter and stud bays packed with cellulose insulation. The first-floor deck was insulated with 10 in. of fiberglass to complete the envelope.

For heat, we couldn't use a hydronic baseboard system because we lacked wall space. A radiant-floor system was more than our budget would allow. Low- and medium-velocity air systems were out because we didn't have space to fit the ductwork. A high-velocity hyrdronic air system with narrow, easily installed ductwork was best for our design and budget issues.

An oil-fired induced-draft direct-venting boiler heats domestic hot water and delivers heat for the air system. The proof of energy efficiency is in the pudding. In our first year, we spent $240 for heat and hot water, $500 for electricity at 12¢ per kilowatt-hour and $35 for propane (used for cooking).

Mike Guertin is a custom home builder and remodeler in East Greenwich, Rhode Island. He is a contributing editor to *Fine Homebuilding* magazine and co-author of *Precision Framing* (The Taunton Press, Inc., 2001) and author of *Roofing with Asphalt Shingles* (The Taunton Press, Inc., 2002).

Downsizing with Style

THE WORDS "SIMPLIFY, SIMPLIFY ...," WHICH HENRY DAVID Thoreau tried to teach us, seem rarely to apply to architecture or construction in this day and age. But we thought that this project might give us just that opportunity. Our client was happily giving her large, formal, turn-of-the-century house over to her daughter, her son-in-law, and their family.

But this client also had a strong desire to stay on the land that she had lived on and loved for over 50 years. And she wished to live within walking distance of her grandchildren. So as we designed her cottage, just down the hill from her old house and her family, all she told us was to "keep it simple."

Long Drive to a Small Cottage

The cottage shares the same driveway as the main house, rolling across a hayfield and then rising beneath oaks and maples. Just before the driveway curves up to the main house, the drive to the new cottage branches off and follows the contours of a lower field along a stone retaining wall (see photo p. 14) ending in a small courtyard that forms the main entry to the cottage.

The cottage was sited to give our client the same incredible views that she enjoyed from the main house up the hill. The cottage sits on a steeply sloping site, overlooking a large freshwater pond, where a population of ducks and geese provides great music and entertainment. Across the water are farm fields and an apple orchard, and in the distance, salt marshes stretch to a line of sand dunes and the ocean beyond.

A large curved retaining wall inspired by the work of landscape architect Frederick Law Olmsted forces the house out over the slope and closer to the

A simple entry. This simple entry is just a few steps away from a protective breezeway, the garage, and a sturdy rock wall squaring off the courtyard. Photo taken at A in floor plan.

The ceiling material is lightly stained beadboard that conveys the lofty, airy feeling of a summer cottage in Maine.

pond. The wall captures space for an outdoor terrace and makes the living room within feel as if it's sitting at the water's edge. We originally called for the wall to be made of stone, but the scale of the wall and cost of materials turned out to be daunting. Instead, we substituted a stuccoed concrete wall with granite capstones and segmented mahogany railing.

A Small House with a Big Room

When my partner, Sheldon Pennoyer, and I first met with our client, we realized that our challenge was to design a small house that felt generous (see floor plans p. 17). We accomplished this task by creating a main space that is markedly larger than the other spaces in the house both in plan and in section (see photo top facing page). This

great room generates a surprising scale shift inside a small structure.

Comprising the living-room and dining-room spaces, the great room has a high ceiling with exposed rafters and collar ties. The ceiling material is lightly stained beadboard that conveys the lofty, airy feeling of a summer cottage in Maine.

This room sits at the junction of several smaller surrounding spaces, including a small, manageable kitchen (see photo top p. 16) and a separate master-bedroom wing. This centralized plan is designed for simple, easy living.

Full-height windows on the south side of the great room open to a flagstone terrace with an undercut porch that provides the interior with summer shade. The only room in the house separate from the great room is a third bedroom, at the north end of the cottage. This space doubles as a study, or it

ABOVE AND LEFT Great room hub. Lightly stained, exposed beams add to the lofty feeling of the great room that adjoins all the other major spaces in the house. Photo taken at D on floor plan. Built-ins flank the fireplace in the living-room area of the great room. Inset photo taken at E on floor plan.

ABOVE A small, simple kitchen. A doorway and a passthrough to the formal dining area open this small but ample kitchen to the great room. Photo taken at F on floor plan.

RIGHT Hideaway for the grandkids. A bright bedroom tucked under the roof on the second floor is the perfect spot when the grandchildren want to sleep over. Photo taken at G on floor plan.

could provide quarters for a live-in helping hand in future years.

On the second floor, an overlook peeks down into the great room from the end of a wide hallway that is designed as a library. At the other end of the library, the grandchildren's bedroom is tucked under the eaves (see photo above).

CENTRALIZED DESIGN FOR A SIMPLIFIED LIFESTYLE

The great room in this house forms a hub both in scale and in location for the rest of the house. All the rooms except for the study/spare bedroom in the back of the house have direct access to this large two-story space. To keep the scale of the house down, the garage was built separately but connected to the house by a covered breezeway.

SPECS

BEDROOMS: **3**

BATHROOMS: **3**

SIZE: **2,400 sq. ft.**

COST: **n/a**

COMPLETED: **1999**

LOCATION: **Ipswich, Massachusetts**

ARCHITECT: **O'Neil Pennoyer Architects (Russell Campaigne, Project Architect)**

BUILDER: **Robert Weatherall and Co.**

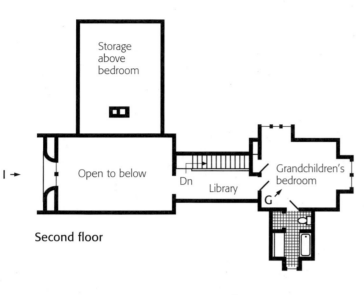

Second floor

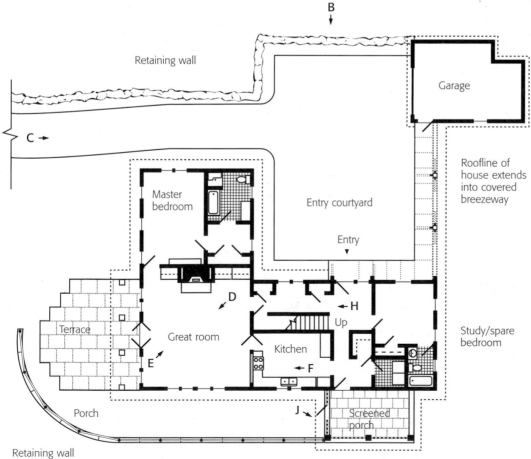

North

0 2 4 8 ft.

Photos taken at lettered positions.

First floor

All aboard! A depot-style breezeway supported by gracefully curved timbers affords protected access to a separate garage (photo taken at B on floor plan) while creating a courtyard for the main entry to the house.

As the project took shape, we learned that achieving simplicity can be complex.

The Amtrak Breezeway

To maintain the scale of a real cottage, we separated the garage from the house. But to ensure easy, safe access to the garage, we designed a covered breezeway.

The breezeway leads directly to the main entry of the house rather than coming off a back door, as it would in larger houses. This arrangement preserves the old-world formality of entering the house via the main entry, rather than sneaking in the back way.

The breezeway connection to the garage also creates an entry courtyard (see photo above). We wanted to shape an intimate arrival space both welcoming and secure in the tradition of the English garden courtyard. Here, cars and flower gardens happily coexist.

A timber arcade with curved brackets supports the breezeway like an open umbrella in a manner reminiscent of a railroad platform. The timbers frame views of the pond and distant landscapes. But unlike the main house up the hill, these views are enjoyed from the relative comfort of the protected outdoor courtyard.

LEFT Recessed curves in wood and copper. The curved walls and flashing for this recessed window that has been built into the space above the porch required the touch of a special craftsman. Photo taken at I on floor plan.

BELOW Private screening. A secluded screened-in porch in the back of the house appears to be in the tops of the trees that overlook the pond below. Photo taken at J on floor plan.

Basic Materials Speak for Themselves

The guiding principle we used for detailing this project was that simple volumes were inherently beautiful, and with appropriate refinement, they would give the cottage all the expression it needed.

The steeply pitched roof with its deep overhang reflects the slope of the land and conveys a surprising feeling of weight for a structure of this size. But the subtle curve at the eaves and the narrow trim line add an equally surprising note of spirited lightness. The classical pediment over the porch curves inward to a recessed central window, adding depth to the structure (see photo top p. 19). In the private screened porch off the rear of the house, heavy wooden columns create a feeling of safety and security where the grade drops to the pond below (see photo bottom p. 19).

The Paradox of Simplicity

As the project took shape, we learned that achieving simplicity can be complex. We also realized that once a project goes from design to construction, the burden of accomplishing this goal shifts from architect to contractor. We were fortunate to have Robert Weatherall as the general contractor for this project. Bob and his crew not only understood the intent of the design, but they worked closely with Russell Campaigne, the project architect, playing an active role in further refining and realizing our goals.

The flared eaves and the curved soffits that sweep up to frame the pediment required the skills and care of a boatbuilder. Bob's crew flared the shingles at the base of the sidewalls using triple courses of shingles, then made custom jambs and casings for the doors and windows to match the flare of the shingles.

The exposed framing on the great-room ceiling was planed from rough lumber to leave crisp edges. The ceiling was then overlaid with a secondary rafter system to provide space for insulation and airflow.

Bob built the stair balustrade (see photo facing page), as well as the countertops for built-ins in the living room, of wood gleaned from an ancient elm that had died on the property. The richly colored wood stands as a tribute to a grand old tree, and it gave us an opportunity to use local materials.

David O'Neil is a partner in O'Neil Pennoyer Architects (www.op-architects.com), an architectural firm in Groton, Massachusetts.

An old friend lives on. The rich wood for the balustrade in this stairway came from a deceased elm tree that once provided a shady spot on the site. Photo taken at H on floor plan.

A Basic Box Isn't All Bad

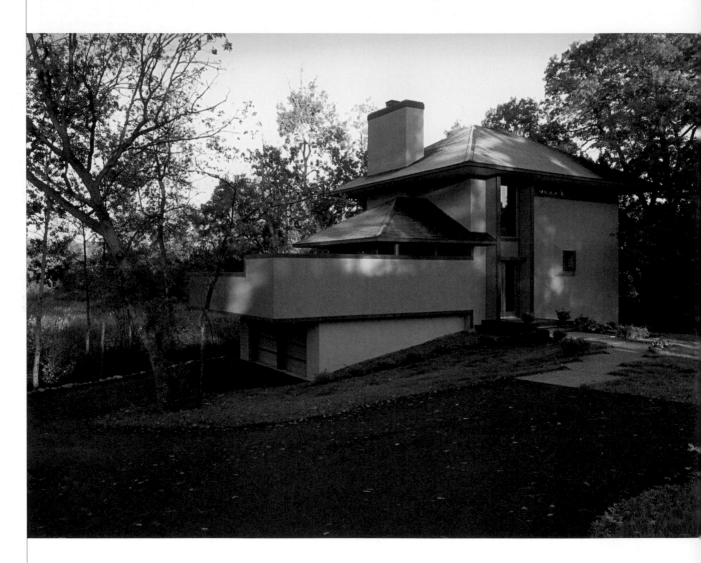

BACK IN THE '60S, A POPULAR TUNE CONDEMNED THE EVILS OF suburban sprawl in the singsong lyric "little boxes on the hillside." Then, as now, the word *box* conjures an image of the most unimaginative, poorly constructed type of houses.

However, in a house I recently completed for Bill Stump, a musician and good friend of mine, I found that working inside a simple box, or cube, created satisfying spaces and lent itself naturally to dynamic views both inside and outside the house. And without the jogs and angles that clutter so many "well-designed" houses, Bill's house was a lot more economical to build. The site borders a wetland wildlife refuge, so we named the house Marshside.

Welcome to the cube. Morning light filters into the house through two-story glazing in the main entry. The attached garage with porch and deck above disguises the cube shape of the house. Photo taken at A on floor plan.

ABOVE A kitchen on the side. A high peninsula and low ceiling separate the private kitchen areas from the open, dynamic dining-room and living-room spaces. Photo taken at E on floor plan.

LEFT Two-story dining room. A 16-ft. ceiling and windows on two levels make the dining room the most dramatic and spacious spot in the house. Photo taken at C on floor plan.

Ceiling Heights Help to Break Down the Box

At less than 50 sq. ft., the entry to the house isn't huge, but I designed it to establish the house's character. The 8-ft.-high entrance doors extend a generous welcome, and the full glazing gives arriving guests a glimpse of the interior (see photo facing page).

With the entry enclosed on three sides and situated between the lower level and the main level of the house, there are no clues to the geometric simplicity of the house.

I conceived the main level as a single, fluid space that comprises the living, dining, and kitchen areas of the home. A variety of ceiling heights and built-in cabinetry

A variety of ceiling heights and built-in cabinetry help to define specific activity areas.

A living room connected to the outdoors. Strong horizontal lines from the light box overhead, the open shelf into the entry, the mantel, and the ceiling trim all draw the eye to the vistas outside the glass doors. Photo taken at D on floor plan.

help to define specific activity areas and again to disguise the basic rectangular nature of the space.

I divided the main floor into introverted and extroverted spaces. The kitchen (see photo right p. 23) is separated from other areas by a 44-in.-high L-shaped peninsula that screens kitchen activities while allowing sight lines to the living and dining area. The only windows in the kitchen are two glass blocks between the countertop and the upper cabinets. At 7 ft., the ceiling gives this part of the kitchen an intimate feeling.

A band of wood trim with built-in light boxes borders the kitchen ceiling for a transition into the most dramatic part of the house, the dining area (see photo left p. 23). Here, the ceiling reaches upward 16 ft. with glazing on two sides. The lower windows allow views to the marshland, and the upper windows look into the tops of the trees behind the house.

When seated at the built-in bench along the north wall of the dining area, Bill gets an unexpected view into the house's upper level. Wood trim set out from the wall encircles the dining area at header height above 8-ft. sliding-glass doors. Along with a cased wooden beam above the dining table, these elements break up the vertical feeling of this space.

Living Room Beckons to the Outdoors

The light-box trim continues unbroken into the living-room area just below the 8-ft. ceiling height (see photo below). Seating is arranged around the fireplace and a built-in entertainment-center cabinet. The living-room area has a more human scale like the kitchen, but the space is filled with light from a series of 8-ft.-tall sliding-glass doors.

Wraparound deck and screened-in porch for summer enjoyment. A deck with a screened-in porch runs the length of the house and over the garage to extend the living and dining areas to the outdoors. Photo taken at B on floor plan.

The glass doors connect the living room visually to the expanse of the marsh, letting the site become an integral part of the interior space. A small cantilevered balcony from the floor above frames one view and also helps to carry the eye from the living room to the outdoors.

Just outside the glass doors, a deck runs the entire length of the house and continues on to a large roof deck above the garage (see photo p. 25). Along with the deck, a roomy screened-in porch expands the living areas during the summer months, yet it is out of sight and out of the way during the long, cold Minnesota winters.

A Study on the Landing

As an architect, I'm always on the lookout for chances to use small nooks and spaces that might be overlooked and wasted. The study at Marshside is a case in point (see photo below).

Midway between the main and upper levels of the house, this quiet little spot occupies the stairway landing above the entry. Measuring only 8 ft. by 9 ft., the study nonetheless has a strong spatial presence. With no doors in the study, views extend both up and down the stairs into the house. A 6-ft. by 8-ft. panel of fixed glass beside the built-in desk, the 10-ft. ceiling and a peek-through opening into a dressing area a half-floor above all add to the three-dimensional richness of this spot.

A Bedroom in the Trees

On the upper level, Bill wanted the main bedroom to impart the feeling of being in a tree house. Marshside was designed for one or two people, so the need for interior doors or complete acoustical separation was not a priority. Because I had this type of flexibility when designing, Bill's bedroom feels significantly larger and more dramatic than it appears on a floor plan.

I'm always on the lookout for chances to use small nooks and spaces that might be overlooked and wasted.

Landing becomes a study. Using the available space on the landing above the entry, a built-in desk creates a private study area. Photo taken at F on floor plan.

SIMPLE LINES INSIDE A RECTANGLE

With the outside of this house shaped like a basic cube, the inside plans become simple rectangles. Interior partitions are strategically placed to afford long lines of sight. The study and entry fall between levels, creating spaces with extended views.

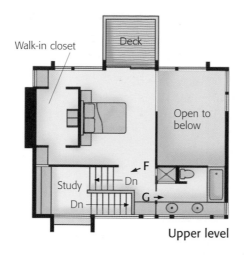

Walk-in closet
Deck
Open to below
Study
Dn
Dn
F
G

Upper level

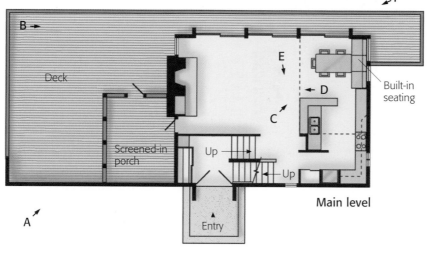

B
Deck
E
D
C
Built-in seating
Screened-in porch
Up
Up
A
Entry

Main level

SPECS

BEDROOMS: 2

BATHROOMS: 2

SIZE: 2,300 sq. ft.

COST: $110.00 per sq. ft.

COMPLETED: 1997

LOCATION: St. Paul, Minnesota

ARCHITECT: Kelly Davis

DESIGNER/BUILDER: Andlar Construction Inc.

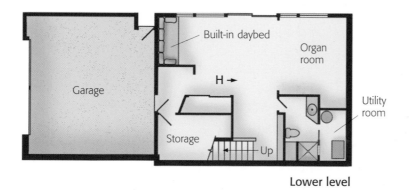

Built-in daybed
Organ room
Garage
H
Utility room
Storage
Up

Lower level

North

0 2 4   8 ft.

Photos taken at lettered positions.

I intentionally kept ceiling heights low around the perimeter of the space, which draws the eye outside to views of a small lake in the marsh. But a higher coved ceiling in the center of the room removes any potential sense of confinement.

Outside the bedroom is a small, private cantilevered deck. To carry the lines of the deck to the indoors, the metal railing continues inside to form the rail on the overlook above the dining area. In addition to the visual connection to the main floor, there are views from the bed to the outside in three different directions.

Bathroom fools the eye. By duplicating architectural elements such as the windows and counter-top on both sides of the glass, an illusion of a mirror is created. Photo taken at G on floor plan.

Soaking Up the View from the Tub

In the main bath, a continuous bank of built-in cabinetry extends from near the top of the stairs in the bedroom along the entire east wall of the bathroom (see photo top left). A glass panel sits atop the cabinet top next to the pocket door into the bathroom. The glass tricks the eye into thinking it's a mirror reflecting symmetrical architectural elements such as the windows and cabinetry.

The final visual surprise occurs at the bathtub. Here another interior window, carefully positioned for privacy, offers the bather views of the treetops and the marsh through the windows in the upper part of the dining room. These views add immeasurably to the pleasure of bathing at Marshside.

A Foundation in Music

The lower level of Marshside is dedicated to music. The largest area of this level is a den with an area that might serve as a guest bedroom for a future owner. For Bill, this space provides the perfect spot for his pipe organ, the centerpiece of the space (see photo top right).

As on the main level, long views and strategically placed glazing expand and extend the sense of space. In one corner, a built-in daybed does double duty for accommodating overnight guests. But the true bonus is that with the open design of the house, music played on the organ filters into the farthest corners of every room.

Kelly Davis is an architect with SALA Architects Inc. in Stillwater, Minnesota.

ABOVE Music in the marsh. A special area on the lower level features the homeowner's pipe organ; the scene outside acts as inspiration. Photo taken at H on floor plan.

LEFT Backyard refuge. All the windows on the west side of this house look onto the marsh that borders the site with beautiful views even on a blustery autumn afternoon. Photo taken at I on floor plan.

In the Belly of the Barn

H OW WOULD YOU LIKE TO DESIGN A 'BAHN' FOR CHARLIE and Monika?" That question introduced our office to this project. At the time, we were nearly done with a renovation of the couple's 80-year-old summer camp, which occupies a waterfront site on Mount Desert Island in midcoast Maine. When the project was started, we were asked to upgrade the facilities as much as possible without spoiling the camp's rustic nature.

Preserving the camp as a camp, however, left some items from Charlie and Monika's wish list unfulfilled. Nearing retirement, Charlie wanted a workshop to pursue boat-building. Their grown children, all musicians, wanted a space for recording and playing. Everyone wanted a winterized space for year-round retreats. We were asked to design a large, flexible structure to satisfy these needs. A two-story barn with a first-floor shop and second-floor living area was the solution (see floor plans p. 37).

'Bring the Light in High and Let It Down Softly'

Our design was inspired by traditional barns from New England and Northern Europe. A native of Sweden, Monika provided us with images of traditional structures from her homeland while we made our own study of the numerous barns on the island. What impressed us most about the Northern European barns were the bold, rustic interiors of the exposed timber-frame structures. Charlie and Monika wanted the new structure to have the same sort of character, but they also wanted plenty of natural light.

Our solution was to funnel natural light into the barn from as many directions as possible, starting from the top. We designed an elongated

Truly a cathedral ceiling. Light streaming in through the overhead monitor windows lends a heavenly glow to the finely crafted timber frame. Photo taken at A on floor plan.

Roof designed for daylighting.
Rising through the peak like an elongated cupola, the monitor bathes the center of the barn with sunlight. Dormers on each end allow windows to illuminate the perimeters. Photo taken at D on floor plan.

cupola called a monitor for the roof (see photo above). As an old architecture professor used to say, the monitor will "bring it in high and let it down softly." Similar to a clerestory, a monitor is a continuous raised section of roof with vertical windows; we used remotely controlled awning windows that promote natural cooling in summer.

Located within the middle two bays of the four-bay timber-frame structure, the monitor bathes the interior of the living space with indirect sunlight (see photo p. 30). Natural lighting is enhanced by the opposing dormers and the large windows on the gable ends that brighten up the perimeters.

The frame was beyond beautiful, and it seemed a shame to cover it up.

Recycled Seaway Timbers Make Up the Frame

The timber frame is recycled Douglas fir that was salvaged from St. Lawrence Seaway "boom stock" (the booms used to corral pulpwood logs destined for Canadian paper mills). The otherwise clear fir was flawed by numerous 1½-in.-dia. iron-stained bolt holes, but Charlie and Monika did not have a problem knowing their timbers had a past, especially because the stains were easily removed with oxalic acid.

For architects whose houses are typically framed with stud walls and trusses, seeing the 12x12 posts and 8x8 primary rafters assembled for the first time was impressive indeed. We arrived for a site visit just after all five bents had been tilted into place and the crew had begun laying the deck for the second floor. When general contractor Scott Werner asked us what we thought, we were speechless. The frame was beyond beautiful, and it seemed a shame to have to cover it up.

Exterior Finishes Help It Blend

We covered the timber frame with a Galvalume® standing-seam metal roof (see Sources). We chose Galvalume for its durability and its fire-resistant qualities as well as its inherent barnlike appearance. The roof is painted dark bronze to help the tall structure blend into the woods.

The siding was designed to break up the vertical dominance of the structure. Board-and-batten western red cedar was installed beneath the overhanging belly band—an extension of the barn-door track cover—with predipped eastern white-cedar shingles

above (see photo below). Another band was created directly below the windowsills by decreasing the course exposure of the shingles.

Because no gutters were used, the roof overhangs were pushed out 30 in. to protect the siding. The gable-end fascia boards are supported with brackets and trusses. With king posts and natural hackmatack knees, the exterior trusses offer visitors a taste of what's inside (see photo p. 30). Traditionally used as lateral bracing in wooden boats, hackmatack knees are harvested locally from the naturally curved trunk-to-root portion of the eastern larch (hackmatack) tree. Our knees were supplied by Newman's Knees of St. Albans, Maine.

Timber Frames Determine Interior Layout

The sliding garage door has a pedestrian door cut into it, but the formal entry is along the side of the barn. To enhance the lofty feeling of the exposed frame, we wanted the approach to the second floor to be somewhat constricted. You enter the first floor via a small mudroom with a relatively low (8 ft. 6 in.) ceiling. Straight ahead is the shop; a right turn leads up the stairs.

The four-bay timber frame dictated the second-floor layout. The bedroom and stair occupy the first bay. The bedroom is separated from the stairwell by a partition wall with a large decorative window (see photo top facing page). The window is just above eye level in the stairwell, which helps to maintain privacy yet allows sunlight from the dormer window to flood the bedroom. The bedroom walls were built high enough for visual privacy but low enough to leave the barn's timber-frame ceiling open from front to back.

The bathroom shares the second bay with the kitchen. The galley-type kitchen

Exterior finishes diminish an imposing structure. Board-and-batten western red cedar covers the first floor; eastern white-cedar shingles cover the second floor. Photo taken at C on floor plan.

LEFT **Light and privacy.** A partition wall with a window separates the bedroom from the stairwell. The west wall of the bathroom sets the bedroom apart from the rest of the barn. Photo taken at B on floor plan.

BELOW **Expansive living and dining space.** Fitting bedroom, bathroom and kitchen spaces within the first two bays of the four-bay timber frame leaves half of the barn wide open for entertaining. Photo taken at E on floor plan.

Creative deception. Designed to resemble Craftsman-style light fixtures, a custom-built cover conceals the heating system's intake and exhaust pipes. Photo taken at F on floor plan.

Originally, the formal entrance of the house was on the other side of the barn. After the framing and mechanical work was done, however, Monika asked that we move the entrance. We were glad to accommodate her, but moving the entrance meant that the intake and exhaust pipes for the high-efficiency propane boiler would be the first items to greet visitors on their way into the barn.

Rather than relocate the heating equipment, we decided to cover the pipes. We designed a cover that would resemble the Craftsman-style exterior-lighting fixtures and had Vulcan Supply of Westford, Vermont, fabricate the cover from 20-oz. lead-coated copper (see photo left). The lead coating protects the copper from corrosive exhaust gases. The cover is lined with copper insect screening that can be left to tarnish or be replaced from time to time if the owners prefer a cleaner look. The wood trim along the bottom edge of the cover was added to protect visitors from sharp edges.

SOURCES

(GSP) Galvalume Sheet Producers of North America
(360) 750-5791
www.steelroofing.com

Newman's Knees
281 Hartland Road
St. Albans, ME 04971
(207) 938-2380
info@newmansknees.com

Vulcan Supply Corp.
P.O. Box 100
Westford, VT 05494
(800) 659-4732
info@vulcansupply.com

leads into the living and dining "great room" space, which occupies the third and fourth bays (see photo bottom p. 35).

You Like Wood, Don't You?

Not surprisingly, the exposed timber frame serves as the focal point for the interior finish strategies. The plank floors, the wainscoting in the stairwell, and the interior slab doors were all milled from the same stock as the frame. The doors are hung with handcrafted strap hinges. The cabinets were also custom-built using recycled fir. The contractor stockpiled vertical-grain lumber for the rails and stiles of the cabinets to ensure stability of the frames.

Other woods were used to lend contrast. A 2-in.-thick slab of Pennsylvania cherry serves as the countertop for the kitchen peninsula. The knotty-pine walls and ceilings (along with the hackmatack knees) balance nicely with the honey-colored fir frame.

First Floor Is an Empty Slate

Although it takes up nearly three-quarters of the first floor, the shop (see photo facing page) was left empty for Charlie and Monika to fill as they approach their retirement. The only requirements they gave us for the shop were that it be well lighted, have 10-ft. ceilings, and have room to store

WIDE-OPEN SPACES FOR WORK AND PLAY

Intended as a year-round refuge to augment the family's nearby summer camp, the barn's open floor plan keeps everything bright and versatile. The first floor has plenty of room for boat-building and winter storage. The second floor is designed for family gatherings and year-round retreats.

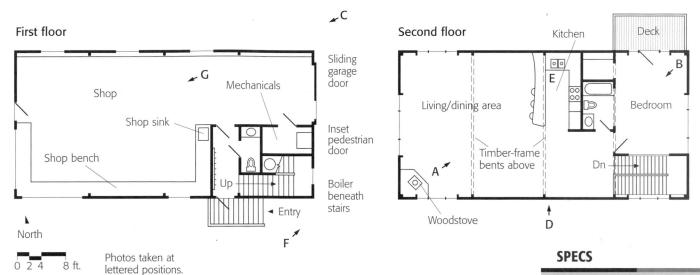

First floor

Shop
Mechanicals
G
Shop sink
Shop bench
Up
Entry
North
0 2 4 8 ft.
Photos taken at lettered positions.

C
Sliding garage door
Inset pedestrian door
Boiler beneath stairs
F

Second floor

Kitchen
Deck
Living/dining area
E
B
Bedroom
Timber-frame bents above
A
Dn
Woodstove
D

SPECS

BEDROOMS: 1
BATHROOMS: 1½
SIZE: 2,304 sq. ft.
COST: n/a
COMPLETED: 1999
LOCATION: Mt. Desert Island, Maine
ARCHITECT: Brian Reading, William McHenry Architects
DESIGNER/BUILDER: Scott Werner
TIMBER-FRAMER: John Connolly & Co.

Almost a blank slate. Although the shop is currently used only for winter storage, the lonely planer will have plenty of company once the owner retires and is able to pursue his boat-building hobby full time. Photo taken at G on floor plan.

a car during the winter months. We satisfied the lighting criteria with a generous mix of windows and incandescent and fluorescent lighting. The oversize windows along the northeast corner are larger versions of the windows that are in Charlie and Monika's beloved waterside camp. The floors are 2x6 tongue-and-groove spruce, the walls are local rough-sawn pine, the ceiling is painted drywall, and the 20-in. planer is made by Powermatic.

Licensed architect Brian Reading of Bangor, Maine has worked for William McHenry Architects in Blue Hill, Maine since 1995.

A Rustic Country Cottage

FOR ALMOST A CENTURY, OREGONIANS HAVE WITNESSED countless truckloads of fir trees, cedars, pines, and spruces hightailing down the highway to a date with a sawmill. The parade has slowed some, and the logs are tiny compared with those of the past. Hundreds of mills have closed as lumber and plywood have been replaced by oriented strand board from the Southeast.

West of Eugene, however, a new agricultural crop has come to life on hills formerly covered with coastal forest. It turns out that Oregon has some wine-growing regions that rank with the best in the world. Ed King III saw this potential back in 1991, and since then, he has been building a first-rate vineyard and winery in Oregon's Lorane Valley. King Estate Winery attracts a steady flow of business associates and family, and they need a place to stay on their visits.

The cottage is an eclectic combination of stylistic features. Its curving roof lends an English country cottage feel to it. But it also uses the sorts of natural materials found in Arts and Crafts houses. For example, the house has resawn fir beams and brackets, and a base and chimney of quarried limestone. Walls are finished with western red-cedar board-and-batten siding combined with cedar wall shingles in the gable ends. A slatelike composition roofing completes the exterior. Although there are drywall surfaces inside, the interior has pine ceilings in some spaces, along with pine soffits, wainscoting, and divided-light windows.

Designing a Modest Great Room

At 1,280 sq. ft., the house is not large. But it includes two private bedrooms with two full baths (see floor plan p. 43). A little more than half of the downstairs is a great room that includes a sitting area, a small kitchen, and a dining alcove (see photo left p. 42). This space is not large, but it feels roomy and functions well because it has a high ceiling and because each portion of the room is sized to accommodate its purpose, although without any wasted space.

Unpretentious façade. Simple gables clad in stone and cedar compose the unpretentious facade. Photo taken at A on floor plan.

The sitting arrangement. A bank of windows overlooking the terrace helps to keep the great room's modest sitting area from feeling cramped. Photo taken at B on floor plan.

The great room includes space for sitting, cooking, and dining. Roof trusses in the big downstairs room lower the perceived height of the ceiling and add another level of detail. Photo taken at E on floor plan.

To pare the floor plan to its minimum, we started with the sitting area in front of the fireplace. At roughly 15 sq. ft., the sitting area is about as small as it can be without feeling cramped. It can be this modest in size for a couple of reasons. First, the sitting area is at the end of the room, without circulation corridors and doorways to complicate matters. Second, the 2-ft.-deep nook on the north side of the room makes a space for a small couch. That extra 2 ft.

leaves enough space between the couch and the big sofa for a suitable passageway. Finally, the terrace along the south side is easily viewed through the bank of windows, visually extending the living space beyond the walls of the house.

A small island counter with cooktop separates the kitchen from the dining area. The key was to allow enough space between the island and the table for two people to pass comfortably when the stools are against the

> *A high ceiling immediately says the room is somehow special.*

A B O V E The dining alcove.
Fold back the French doors to open the dining area to the terrace when the weather gets good. Photo taken at D on floor plan.

ABOVE The other dining alcove. Sunbaked concrete pavers tile the terrace, where a deep roof overhang protects the great room from overheating in the summer. Photo taken at C on floor plan.

On warm, sunny days, the French doors on the south wall can be pivoted flush to their sidelites, opening the table to the terrace and the view of the pond.

island and the chairs are tucked at the table (see photo p. 41). The magic number is 4 ft.

The rule of thumb in our office has always been to allow, typically, 3 ft. 6 in. between a kitchen counter and a kitchen island. The exception is a kitchen such as this one. It's a guest house, after all, with a small kitchen that will be used intermittently to prepare meals for just a few people. In this situation, a 3-ft.-wide passage running between the sink counter and the island is enough. Ironically, within a year of the house's completion, the kitchen was being used by a pair of chefs as their set for a cooking show on the local PBS station.

A dining alcove completes the third function of the great room. In use, it borrows space from the passageway next to the island. On warm, sunny days, the French doors on the south wall can be pivoted flush to their sidelites, opening the table to the terrace and the view of the pond.

When the weather gets pleasant, the terrace is the nicest place to have a dining table (see photo top right). The prevailing breezes are from the west, so the terrace is on the southeast corner of the house, where it is sheltered from the wind by the second-story bedroom.

Pretend Trusses Provide Detail and Intimacy

Putting a high ceiling in a room presents a seemingly contradictory challenge. On the one hand, the eye likes to wander along the sloped planes in a cathedral ceiling. Because most ceilings are 8 ft. high and flat, a high ceiling immediately says the room is somehow special. But there is risk, too. A high ceiling in a small room can make you feel like you're standing at the bottom of a tall box because the scale is all wrong.

In the guest cottage, the great room is 15 ft. wide, and the ceiling is 16 ft. high. The bottoms of the collar ties, which serve a structural purpose in this house, are at 10 ft. The collar ties bring the perceived height of the ceiling down to a comfortable level. But they aren't enough. The big triangular space above the collar ties seems empty and unresolved. Solution: We made the collar ties into the bottom chords of simulated trusses that have 4x4 king posts and diagonal web members (see drawings p. 44). These additional components break up the space into triangles that are related in shape and echo the overall form of the roof at a different scale. The result is a lofty ceiling that has pleasing, structurally plausible shapes and still has a sense of intimacy.

Our builder, Mark Dorman, came up with a clever way to deal with the potential quagmire of fussy trim cuts that it would take to get the ceiling boards to fit tight between the faux trusses. He cut ¾-in. rabbets along the top chords of each truss, providing a notch along each edge to hide the ends of the ceiling boards (see drawing bottom left p. 44). That allowed each board to be cut a little long, and we didn't have to worry about gaps showing up if they weren't just right.

THE INS AND OUTS GIVE THIS PLAN LIFE

Nooks, bump-outs, and alcoves add strategic bits of living space to the inside of this cottage. On the outside, the corners make for interesting jogs, shadowlines, and roof overhangs.

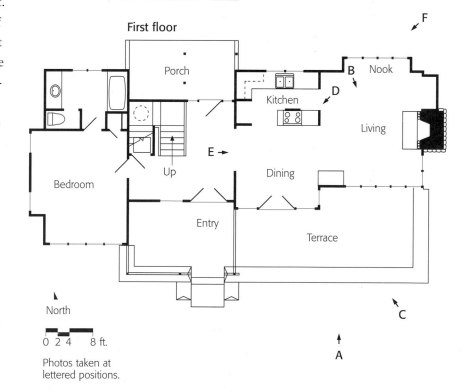

Second floor

First floor

North

0 2 4   8 ft.

Photos taken at lettered positions.

SPECS

BEDROOMS: 2

BATHROOMS: 2

SIZE: 1,288 sq. ft.

COST: n/a

COMPLETED: 1994

LOCATION: Coburg, Oregon

ARCHITECTS: David Edrington and Rob Thallon

DESIGNER/BUILDER: Dorman Construction

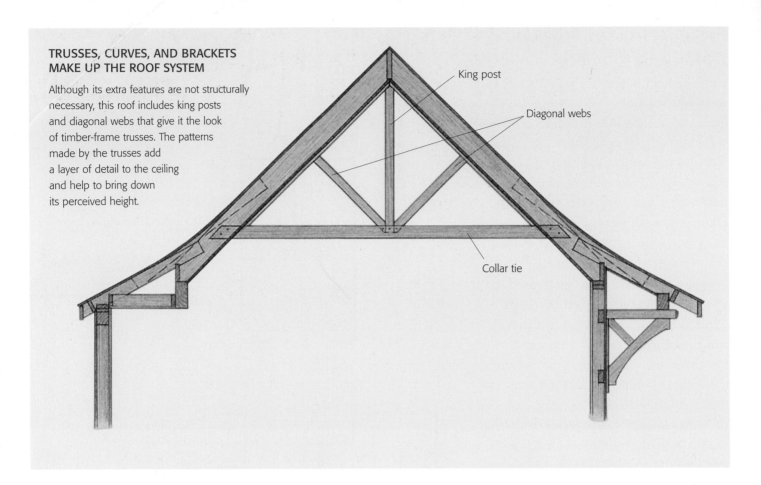

TRUSSES, CURVES, AND BRACKETS MAKE UP THE ROOF SYSTEM

Although its extra features are not structurally necessary, this roof includes king posts and diagonal webs that give it the look of timber-frame trusses. The patterns made by the trusses add a layer of detail to the ceiling and help to bring down its perceived height.

King post

Diagonal webs

Collar tie

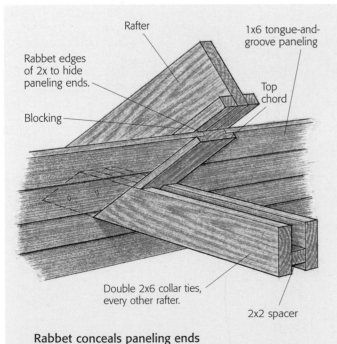

Rafter

1x6 tongue-and-groove paneling

Rabbet edges of 2x to hide paneling ends.

Top chord

Blocking

Double 2x6 collar ties, every other rafter.

2x2 spacer

Rabbet conceals paneling ends

Top chords milled from 2x stock ripped to 4½ in. wide are nailed to the bottoms of the rafters. The 1x6 paneling tucks into the ¾-in. rabbets along the edges of the top chords.

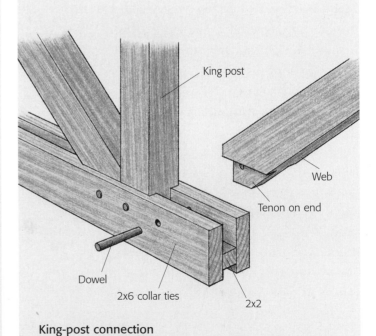

King post

Web

Tenon on end

Dowel

2x6 collar ties

2x2

King-post connection

Every other rafter gets a pair of collar ties, which are separated by a 2x2. The king posts and webs have tenons on their lower ends, which are pinned by dowels to the collar ties. Their upper ends are simply toenailed in place.

The Curve in the Roof

Although the pleasing swoop of the roof is reason enough to build it, the curve is also practical (see photo above). At a 12-in-12 pitch, most of the roof is steep. We wanted 3-ft. 6-in. deep eaves on the south side of the house to shield the living area from the summer sun and to protect the weather side of the house. If the eaves stayed at the same steep pitch as the roof, they would have blocked the windows and presented serious head-banging hazards.

The roof changes pitch a little above the point at which the collar ties are affixed to the rafters. The eave rafters join the main rafters by way of splices made from 2x12s with 20-ft. 6-in. radii curves cut into them (see drawing right). At their outboard ends, the eave rafters are supported by a beam held aloft by curving timber-frame brackets.

David Edrington is an architect practicing in Eugene, Oregon. He designed the cottage with his partner, Rob Thallon.

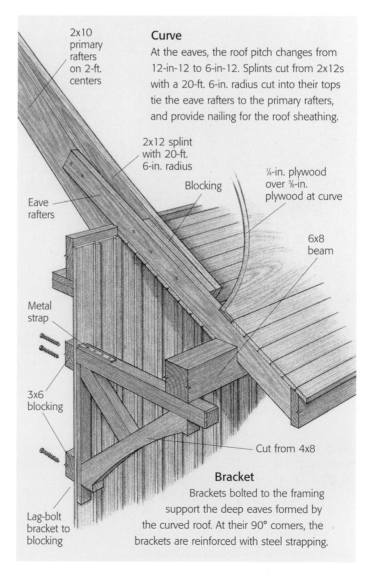

2x10 primary rafters on 2-ft. centers

Curve
At the eaves, the roof pitch changes from 12-in-12 to 6-in-12. Splints cut from 2x12s with a 20-ft. 6-in. radius cut into their tops tie the eave rafters to the primary rafters, and provide nailing for the roof sheathing.

2x12 splint with 20-ft. 6-in. radius

Blocking

¼-in. plywood over ⅜-in. plywood at curve

6x8 beam

Eave rafters

Metal strap

3x6 blocking

Cut from 4x8

Bracket
Brackets bolted to the framing support the deep eaves formed by the curved roof. At their 90° corners, the brackets are reinforced with steel strapping.

Lag-bolt bracket to blocking

A House Designed by Consensus

B Y THE END OF 1994, RALEIGH, NORTH CAROLINA, ARCHITECT Jeff Davis had been successfully designing residential and commercial projects for 20 years. But nothing could have prepared him for his first meeting with future residents of Eno Commons. Instead of sitting down with a single client, Davis faced a group of 15. All of them had ideas—not necessarily the same ones—on what would make the ideal house in the 22-lot community they were planning. Davis was about to be introduced to cohousing, where everything from floor plans to parking would be decided by consensus.

Cohousing, or collaborative housing, is an idea borrowed from Denmark. Although approaches vary, cohousing projects are a mix of private and common land and buildings. Unlike more typical housing developments, where personal connections between residents are left to chance, cohousing projects are designed from the start to foster close relationships. At Eno Commons (named for a river just down the hill), residents organized by developer Sherri Zann Rosenthal own their lots and self-contained houses. But they also get a kitchen-equipped commons house where they can meet for communal meals several times a week, a shared workshop and garden, and a deeper sense of community than they had found elsewhere (see sidebar p. 51).

For Davis, being the project architect involved a lot of listening. Residents set bedrock design approaches. Houses were to be economical, be efficient, be easy to care for, use energy sparingly, and be in keeping architecturally with the area. Finding the process "laborious and sometimes painful," Davis delivered plans that largely satisfied his clients. For about $65 per sq. ft. in building costs, residents could choose among three basic house types measuring 962 sq. ft., 1,483 sq. ft., or 1,974 sq. ft.

Cohousing projects. Like many cohousing projects, this one in Durham, North Carolina, offers residents the benefits of communal living with the privacy of self-contained houses.

ABOVE **Master bedroom on the first floor.** This ground-floor bedroom will make it easier for owners to stay in the house as they grow older. Photo taken at C on floor plan.

A Floor Plan That Accommodates Residents of All Ages

Jessie Handforth Kome and her husband, Bill Davis, live in a four-bedroom "B House," the largest of the versions Davis designed (see photo p. 46). Comfortable now for the couple and their two children, the house also is designed to accommodate them as they get older. A poured-concrete floor flows from one room to the next uninterrupted by interior door sills, handy for anyone using a wheelchair. Although their house includes three bedrooms on the second floor, the couple could easily live on the first floor should they find it difficult to manage the stairs. A first-floor master bedroom (see photo top left) has easy access to an adjacent bathroom and powder room.

ABOVE **Kitchen is compact but has a view.** A small kitchen is separated from the living and dining area by a high counter. Photo taken at D on floor plan.

RIGHT **South-facing windows help to heat the house.** Concrete floors soak up thermal energy in winter while moderating heat in summer. Photo taken at E on floor plan.

Like other houses at Eno Commons, the Davis-Kome place doesn't waste much floor space. Only a few square feet is given over to hallways. The largest space in the house is a 30-ft.-long room that combines all the essentials—a compact kitchen (see photo bottom left facing page), living room and dining area. It ends at a south-facing bank of windows (see photo bottom right facing page) that overlooks the communal meadow and orchard and a door opening to a small rear porch.

A key design concern was making the community a safe place for children. With vehicles relegated to perimeter parking areas, the main drag through the center of Eno Commons is a wide footpath where children can play safely. Windows facing the path from the kitchen, first-floor study, and dining area make it easy for parents to keep an eye on their kids, and a covered front porch a few feet from the footpath encourages contact with neighbors.

Exteriors Have a Regional Feel

Limited to only a few floor plans, the houses at Eno Commons complement each other without looking identical. Central to the community's homey feel are house exteriors that reflect typical North Carolina building traditions (see photo top p. 50). Houses make the most of simple gabled shapes, with clapboard siding on the first floor and board-and-batten siding on the second floor (both are low-maintenance fiber-cement products).

Exterior trim is simple. The 8-in-12 roofs are covered with galvanized-steel panels, a regional favorite. Simple porch railings and pickets are made of pressure-treated southern yellow pine, and porch floors, like those inside, are poured concrete.

It wasn't enough that Eno Commons houses were economical to build. They also

Cohousing projects are designed from the start to foster close relationships.

PLANNING A NEIGHBORHOOD FROM SCRATCH

Eno Commons, a cohousing development near Durham, North Carolina, was designed as a mix of shared and private holdings where vehicles are limited to the perimeter. A commons house, a vegetable garden, and an orchard are owned in common. Houses come with simple floor plans and are energy efficient and barrier-free.

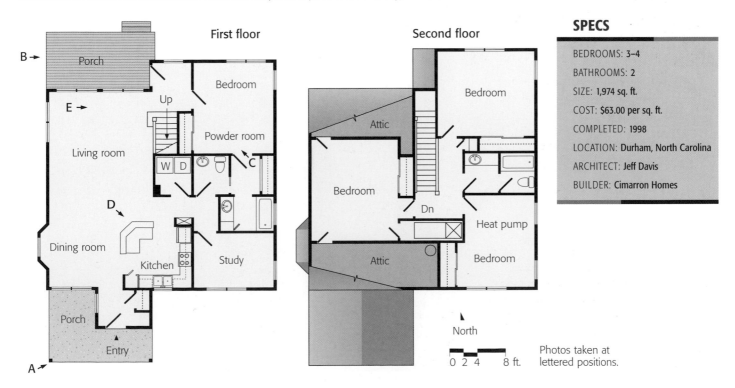

First floor

B → Porch
E →
Up
Living room
Bedroom
Powder room
W D
C
Dining room
D
Kitchen
Study
Porch
Entry
A →

Second floor

Attic
Bedroom
Bedroom
Dn
Heat pump
Attic
Bedroom

North

0 2 4   8 ft.

Photos taken at lettered positions.

SPECS

BEDROOMS: **3–4**
BATHROOMS: **2**
SIZE: **1,974 sq. ft.**
COST: **$63.00 per sq. ft.**
COMPLETED: **1998**
LOCATION: **Durham, North Carolina**
ARCHITECT: **Jeff Davis**
BUILDER: **Cimarron Homes**

ABOVE Houses have a regional flavor. Gabled shapes, metal roofs, and simple trim keep houses in tune with the architectural aesthetics of the region. Photo left taken at A on floor plan; photo above taken at B on floor plan.

had to be cheap to run. Last July and August, two unusually steamy months even for North Carolina, Davis and Kome paid an average of $55 a month for lights, domestic hot water, and air conditioning (houses also have electric ranges). Energy efficiency revolves around three strategies: a passive-solar design, a geothermal heat pump, and a tightly sealed building envelope.

Eaves over south-facing windows are designed so that they allow sunlight to pass into the house in winter. Some of the heat is soaked up by the concrete floor and the tons of stone beneath it. When the sun is higher in the sky during the summer, the eaves block more of the sunlight and heat.

Consultants from the Advanced Energy Corporation in Raleigh wrote the specifications on heating and cooling, ductwork, and detailing the building envelope. According to Arnie Katz, a building-science specialist there, an effective air barrier between conditioned and unconditioned

spaces was crucial. An interior vapor barrier was required by code. Katz says blower-door tests found that air leaks in Eno Commons houses were significantly below those of typical new housing in the region.

Heating systems rely on underground loops of high-density polyethylene tubing that keep water circulating in the system at a constant 60°F to 65°F. A heat pump tucked under the eaves on the second floor turns that into forced-air heat in the winter and air conditioning in summer, plus heats domestic hot water. The system is very quiet.

A Community Still in the Making

By late 1998, only a half-dozen families had moved into Eno Commons. Construction vehicles, not people, still had priority on the development's dusty central walkway. Foundations for seven of the 22 houses were still to be poured, and the commons building was a weedy piece of vacant ground. Even so, enough of the pieces were in place to get a good sense of what the place eventually will look like.

But Eno Commons was never just about the houses. It was about overcoming social alienation. Davis had realized early on that his architectural success here meant walking away from the project with residents believing they, not he, had been the principal designers. They got just the houses they wanted, but they seemed just as taken with the warm social architecture they had created at the same time.

Scott Gibson, formerly a senior editor at *Fine Homebuilding*, is author of *The Workshop* (The Taunton Press, Inc., 2003).

Central to the community's homey feel are house exteriors that reflect typical North Carolina building traditions.

Building Smaller, for Now

Most of my clients have the same problem: There just isn't enough money to build the house that they want, when they want. To build that dream house, they have to buy the property first, and it usually costs more than they've planned. There's no shame in paying for a great site; if you don't start with a great site, it's harder to end up with a house that you really love. Besides, great sites are a better long-term investment. But it's a real shame if this wonderful site can't be enjoyed because there isn't enough money left over to build the house that you want in the near term. So why not build in phases, something that you can live in now and then use in some manner later on?

The Xanadu Principle

Essentially, you want a condensed design that gives you a starting point for your life on this new bit of land. In some cases, my firm tries to build less than the final project at first to make it work financially. Of course, there are tricks to building in this fashion. The project must be seen as a phased process of what will be built now and what will be built later. When doing phased work, you must carefully consider what I call the transaction cost. In dollar terms, it's simply the difference between the combined costs of phase 1 and phase 2 separately versus the cost of doing the project all at once. A big factor in this difference is the duration of phase 1. If phase 1 lasts a short time, these costs tend to loom large. If you can live in phase 1 for some years, the inefficiency of phasing, as expressed by the added cost, becomes less important.

A small house gets you on the land quickly. Patterned after a nearby boathouse, this house allows the owners to experience their property without building an expensive larger house. Photo taken at A on floor plan.

There's no shame in paying for a great site; if you don't start with a great site, it's harder to end up with a house that you really love.

The biggest problem we've found with phased jobs is that there is a tendency for our clients to invest all their hopes and dreams in phase 1; we refer to this problem as the Xanadu principle. If they start by building a guest house that could grace Xanadu, it may be hard to realize that someday it will need to sit in the shadow of a more modest, if larger, house.

A couple of summers ago, my firm built two interesting houses; each tackled the problem of establishing a residence in the short run that doesn't compromise the final house. These two houses represent different strategies because they were solving two different problems: Do we really want to live here in Maine? And can we afford to live here now?

Strategy 1: Living in the Guest House

The Chapmans weren't really sure how much time they would ultimately spend on their waterfront lot in Maine. One possibility was that they would try summers and, after retirement, live there most of the year. However, they wanted to sample coastal life without committing the money for a year-round three-bedroom house. They had always loved a boathouse down the cove, and we set out to make a smaller version of it that, for now, would work as a small home (see photo p. 53). The result of our design collaboration was a house, unfinished on the inside, that might function in four possible scenarios:

- They could leave it as is and use it infrequently, knowing they had invested the minimum that would allow them to use the land. After some years, they could sell it, not having invested a fortune in the house.
- They could use the land, but only in the summer. If they decided to retire here and build a bigger house on the property (see drawing left), the boathouse would become a summer guest house. We wouldn't need to insulate, drywall the interior, or add a heating system.
- They could use the land both summer and winter. They could plan to retire here and build a bigger house, fully winterizing the boathouse to function as a guest house or an office, or both.
- They could use the land throughout the year, but they could retire somewhere else and decide that the boathouse was really enough house to have on the Maine coast. The owners might winterize it, adding more usable space in the basement, but not build another house.

Treat the Framing Like Finish Work

To maximize these options, we chose a middle course to finish the boathouse. It seemed likely that the house would never be finished beyond this state (for instance,

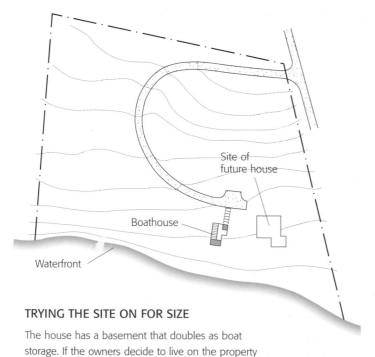

TRYING THE SITE ON FOR SIZE

The house has a basement that doubles as boat storage. If the owners decide to live on the property year-round, they can build a larger house and use the boathouse as a guest house.

Bare-bones design doesn't have to be Spartan. Despite an unfinished interior, careful work, open bookcases, and mini-spotlights all contribute to the casual warmth of the living room. Photo taken at B on floor plan.

it would never be fully insulated), so we made its unfinished interior details look more intentional (see photo above).

Builder Larry Packwood and his crew treated the structural lumber more like trim than framing, sanding off grade stamps and generally paying attention to cosmetic details. These guys do crisp framing anyhow, so we didn't have to emphasize that aspect.

To keep the interior lines clean and open, we framed the roof with pairs of 2x6 rafters on 2-ft. centers. A single rafter tie sandwiched between every other set added some meat to the structure. Normally, we would be concerned about the lack of insulation space that a 6-in. rafter would give us, but if we had to insulate later, we could spend a few extra dollars and spray polyurethane foam for an acceptable R-value.

We sheathed the building in #4 tongue-and-groove pine. The knotty pine looks better from the inside, smells like a summer house, and doesn't let the shingle nails show through. I have always liked pine sheathing because the wall breathes better than plywood, but in this case, it was an aesthetic decision. The extra labor paid to nail it up was worthwhile. We used insulated-glass windows so that we could upgrade the house to year-round living status without replacing the windows, too. Although we didn't trim out the windows, we did attach sills so that the windows would look somewhat finished.

The foundation's exterior was fully insulated with 2 in. of rigid foam; we've found that insulation keeps foundations drier in the summer by minimizing the amount of condensation. It adds an extra $500 or so to the overall cost, but it's an improvement that is tough to add later.

Of course, we had to do all the site work: build the road, bring in the power, dig the septic, and drill the well. These expenses can turn a small house into a pretty pricey affair, even if it is tiny. But that's the price you pay for getting on the land if you have a wild, beautiful place like the Chapmans'.

I have always liked pine sheathing because the wall breathes better than plywood.

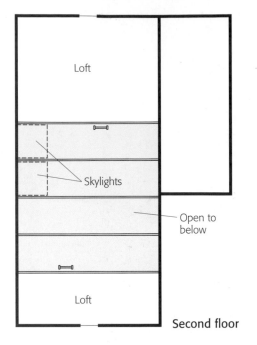

Loft

Skylights

Open to below

Loft

Second floor

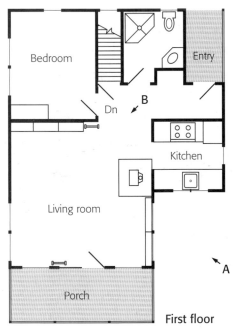

Bedroom

Entry

Dn   B

Kitchen

Living room

Porch

A

First floor

North

0   2   4   8 ft.

Photos taken at lettered positions.

LOFTS ADD SPACE TO A ONE-STORY PLAN

Loft spaces at each end of this compact house plan gave the owners a potential extra bedroom and storage for nonessential items.

SPECS

BEDROOMS: 1

BATHROOMS: 1

SIZE: 648 sq. ft.

COST: $96.00 per sq. ft., excluding site costs

COMPLETED: 1998

LOCATION: Blue Hill, Maine

ARCHITECT: Knight Associates, Architects

BUILDER: Larry Packwood Builders

After adding in the site costs, we arrived at a pretty hefty number. So we decided that to make sense of this level of expenditure, the house should be big enough to include a small bedroom on the main level (the original plan featured sleeping lofts). This strategy would also protect the resale value by giving it much broader market appeal. If you include site-development costs, this house was brutally expensive per square foot to build. But because the house is relatively small, the overall cost is still a great deal less than if the Chapmans had built a "real" house, and they are now reaping the benefits of the cash outlay they made for the land.

Strategy 2: The Living Room Serves as the House

The Nobles were committed to living part of the year in Maine in the near future. Exactly when in the future and how much of the year would work itself out, but the Nobles didn't need the multiple options of the Chapmans. They could not spend the cash or add the debt now for the house that they wanted.

Initially, we had designed a Greek-revival farmhouse that resolved into something that pleased all of us. By our calculations, however, it was going to cost around $350,000. Although that figure was affordable at some point, it wasn't in the cards in the foreseeable future, so why not build just the guest house first?

Although a guest house was part of the final plan, the Nobles wanted to live on the primary site rather than in a corner where a guest house might ordinarily sit. There was really only one great place to build on the site.

We first looked at building a core of the house: kitchen, bathroom, a place to sleep. In practical terms, though, that meant building everything but the living room, and building the most expensive rooms to boot. Another strategy that left spaces unfinished to save money was acceptable to them but was still too expensive. We needed to cut costs at least by half. Simply deleting some interior work could save 10% to 15%, but it wouldn't yield big-enough savings.

With a flash of the brilliance that justifies my big-bucks fees, I thought, "Instead

ABOVE A tiny house is the germ of a larger house. This two-room house provides enough space for the owners until they can add more rooms. When the house is enlarged, the two rooms will become the living room and porch. Photo taken at C on floor plan.

LEFT Living room benefits from big windows and a screened porch. An inexpensive, stripped-down interior shouldn't preclude a good view and plenty of ventilation. Once the essentials are built, the details can be added later. Photo taken at D on floor plan.

Bedroom and Bathroom Addition Unbolts

Built to augment the central living area, the small addition was bolted on to the main structure to make the house's expansion easier. Still intact, the addition could be doubled in size and become the basis for a new guest cottage. The hex nuts were left exposed on the bedroom wall (see photo below) for easy access (see drawing right).

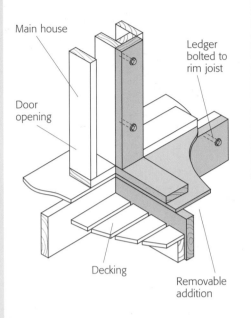

Main house

Door opening

Ledger bolted to rim joist

Decking

Removable addition

LEFT **Exposed bolts make disassembly a snap.** The hex nuts to the right of the bedroom door betray the location of the bolts that connect the addition to the main house. Photo taken at F on floor plan.

of building everything except for the living room, why not build just the living room?"

Actually, the living room included an attached screened porch. We would modify the screened-porch roof so that the living-room space extended over it to form a loft. Extending the roof over the loft would improve the house's roofline. The loft could also be used as an office or as overflow sleeping space, making the living room more flexible in what is still a pretty modest house.

Bolt-on Module Increases Space

Unfortunately, my living-room plan didn't create enough room to make a self-contained living unit. We needed a kitchen, a bathroom, and a bedroom (the Nobles didn't want to climb a ship's ladder to go to bed). Because the living room functions as the kitchen, dining room, entry, and living room during the first phase, we deleted the fireplace and put in a temporary kitchen where the future fireplace chimney would be. For heat, we bought a gas-fired parlor stove.

Half-room at the back is easily removed. The author designed a small addition for the bedroom and bath. When the house is enlarged, the addition can be removed, doubled and used as a guest house. Photo taken at E on floor plan.

To create a bathroom and bedroom, we attached a small room to the back of the house (see photo above). In a future phase, this room will be moved and probably doubled in size to become a guest house. This added section is bolted to the living room and sits on posts anchored to 12-in.-dia. Sonotubes. During phase 2, we will remove the Sonotubes and extend the foundation.

For this project, the transaction costs were low. Minimizing these costs figured prominently in our decision to put a hip roof on the back section. It would have been simpler to extend the living-room gable roof over the back section, but it would have been more difficult to remove

the addition in phase 2. We also didn't want a high gable roof on the final guest house. Instead, we chose a lower-profile hip roof, whose definition emphasizes the over-scale nature of the permanent part and gives it a bit of charm.

Inside (see photo bottom p. 57), we didn't spend money on special framing because we knew that it would be covered with drywall and trim. We did spring for #4 pine tongue-and-groove sheathing boards for the same reasons as in the Chapmans' project.

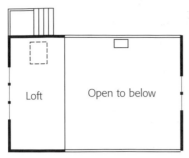

Second floor

CREATING THE BASIC INGREDIENTS OF A HOUSE

During the first phase of building on a relatively expensive lot, the author started with an essential, inexpensive house: a living room with kitchen facilities, a bedroom, and a bath. A loft and screened porch add space and utility. If and when the second phase takes place, the back section can be unbolted and the house enlarged to include a separate kitchen/dining area and a larger bedroom/bath combination.

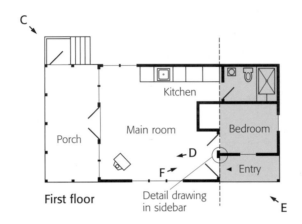

First floor

Detail drawing in sidebar

SPECS

BEDROOMS: **2, including a loft**

BATHROOMS: **1**

SIZE: **700 sq. ft.**

COST: **$114.00 per sq. ft., excluding site costs**

COMPLETED: **1998**

LOCATION: **Brooklin, Maine**

ARCHITECT: **Knight Associates, Architects**

BUILDER: **Larry Packwood Builders**

Removable addition

Phase 1: The basic house

When Unfinished Is Enough

Both clients were disciplined. In the Chapmans' case, we added finishing touches because their boathouse is most likely a permanent situation rather than an incomplete house. In both cases, the exterior was finished to the utmost without compromises, so no upgrading would be necessary later.

Although I see both of these buildings as works in progress, I think they still must have interest as finished objects in the pres-

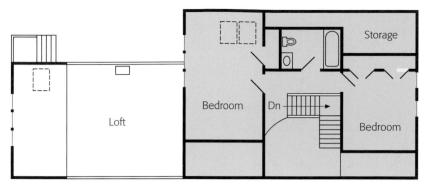

Second floor

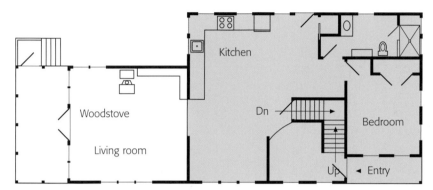

First floor

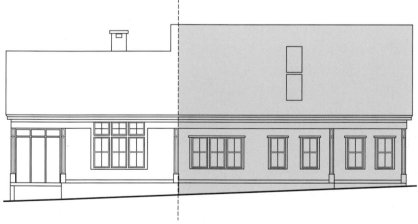

Phase 2: The expanded house

◢ North

0 2 4   8 ft.

Photos taken at lettered positions.

ent so that the owners can feel good about the outlays made to get on the land.

In both cases, we spent less than 50% of the cost of building the final house, and now my clients get to enjoy their land and not be broke. My hope is that after they have lived on the land in these casual wooden cabins, they will be in a better position to make decisions about designing their "real" houses.

Robert Knight is an architect in Blue Hill, Maine. He is the author of *A House on the Water* (The Taunton Press, Inc., 2003).

An Industrial Loft
in Texas

A modern, minimal home on the range. The homeowners wanted an industrial aesthetic. Stucco and Galvalume siding, a geometric shape, and no window trim add a modern face to the neighborhood. Photo taken at B on floor plan.

RIGHT **The ultimate open plan.** The only partition walls are those enclosing bathrooms and a closet behind the bedroom loft, shielded for privacy by an obscured-glass balustrade. Continuing the balustrade in clear glass along the bridge and stairs will preserve sightlines while satisfying code. Photo taken at A on floor plan.

MOST RESIDENTS OF BURLESON, TEXAS, DO NOT ENVISION their hometown as a what's-happening-now hotbed of architectural design. Even so, Mike Young and Gayla LaBry wanted a notably modern home. They had cultivated an appreciation for modern architecture during frequent trips to Europe. The couple wanted an industrial, loftlike feel with exposed steel inside and out. Mike had recently completed a steel addition to his employer's glass-manufacturing company, and he liked the idea of a steel-framed home that would resist fire, termites, and rot.

They found a gently sloping half-acre lot with established oak trees in an unincorporated part of town. The area sported a collection of quirky 1970s homes: a ranch with the brick facade laid in undulating courses and an occasional stone thrown in, builder's-choice neoclassical revivals, even a partially underground home. Here, they could build a unique home without alienating the neighbors.

Building on Piers Combats Expansive Soils

Mike and Gayla come from Louisiana, where elevated houses are a tradition, so they wanted their home raised above grade with a wraparound deck. Raising the small house would make it seem a little more grand and would improve the views to the south. But there were more fundamental reasons for building on piers.

According to the soils test, the site's expansive soils had a potential vertical rise of 9 in. This type of soil, largely clay, expands when wet and shrinks when dry. Placing a slab on grade often results in uneven moisture levels between the soil under and around the slab, which can mean cracked slabs or walls.

A raised pier-and-beam foundation would limit contact with soils and, on this sloping lot, would allow surface water to run under the house. We located 12-in.-dia. concrete piers to carry equal loads; in theory, all the piers should sink or rise the same amount.

Steel Framing Resists Fire, Termites, and Rot

Resting on concrete piers and beams, red iron forms the posts, beams, purlins, and second-story joists (see photo bottom left). Steel in-fill forms the rest of the beams, studs, and joists (see photo bottom right). Sprayed polyurethane followed by fiberglass insulates the structure. Photos taken at B on floor plan.

After the concrete subs poured the piers, they made 12-in.-wide by 24-in.-high reinforced-concrete beams that sit on top of the piers. A 10-ga. steel frame is bolted to the concrete beams; then 3-in. by 3-in. by ⅛-in. steel angles are shot to the beams, and 12-ga. floor joists (8 in. deep) are welded to the steel angles with purlin clips.

Steel Framing Members Come Precut

The steel supplier in Houston, Classic Steel Frame Homes, used my construction drawings to prepare shop drawings for our approval. Then a computer-driven roll-form machine produced the engineered steel frame. The machine cuts flat stock to length, drills the holes, and forms the stock into C-shaped sections that are ready to bolt or screw together. In a matter of days, Classic shipped the entire steel package: frame, purlins, beams, joists, studs, fasteners, roofing, and siding. Upon arrival at the job site, the builder, S & B Construction of Weatherford, Texas, spread out the steel like so many toy parts.

Classic provided a red iron frame that bolted together. Each section of the frame went up as a single bent, as in timber framing, with roof purlins and second-floor joists connecting the bents (see photo bottom left facing page). Come-alongs helped to square the structure before bolts were tightened. The roof decking and standing-seam metal roof act as a diaphragm and impart rigidity to the structure.

After the frame and roof went up, the framing crew installed 1⅛-in. plywood decking; 18-ga., 8-in.-deep exterior-wall studs; windows; glass-block grids; and exterior doors (see photo bottom left facing page). The two-story living-room section was sheathed with ½-in. oriented strand board (OSB), #30 felt, wire lath and stucco. The stacked, single-story spaces (the kitchen and

master suite above) were clad in 26-ga. Galvalume R-panels. Combining two different siding materials outside adds aesthetic interest to the exterior while marking the arrangement of volumes inside.

SPACE, LIGHT, AND TIGHT DESIGN MAKE A SMALL LOFT SEEM BIG

Open space and plenty of light enlarge the small plan, and containing the laundry between the master bath and closet helps to keep that space clutter-free.

SPECS

BEDROOMS: 1

BATHROOMS: 1½

SIZE: 950 sq. ft.

COST: $126.00 per sq. ft.

COMPLETED: 2000

LOCATION: Burleson, Texas

ARCHITECT: Richard Wintersole

BUILDER: S & B Construction

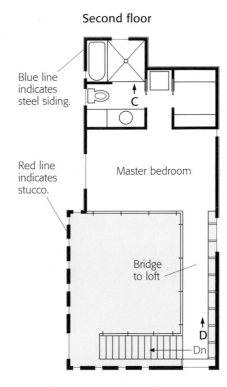

Second floor

Blue line indicates steel siding.

Red line indicates stucco.

Master bedroom

Bridge to loft

C

D

Dn

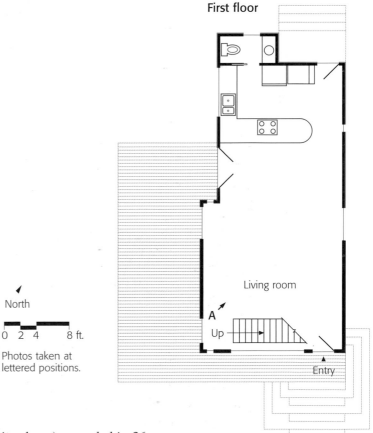

First floor

Living room

North

0 2 4   8 ft.

Photos taken at lettered positions.

A
Up

Entry

B

SOURCES

Classic Steel Frame Homes
7313 Fairview
Houston, TX 77041
(713) 896-7425
www.metalhomes.com

S & B Construction
102 Summer Stone Court
Weatherford, TX 76087
(817) 596-9119
www.sandbconstruction.com

ABOVE A tub in the shower. A deep soaking tub and twin showers combine to make one large bathing area. Photo taken at C on floor plan.

ABOVE A beacon of modernism. Seeing the house at night highlights the geometric design. Photo taken at B on floor plan.

Minimalist Interiors Avoid Clutter

Before moving in, Mike and Gayla looked at all their belongings and took the attitude, "When in doubt, throw it out." That motto would make maintaining an uncluttered living space much easier.

Interior finishes include drywall without crown molding, frameless maple cabinetry, and prefinished wood floors on the first floor. A sandblasted, clear-coated steel stair

An industrial feel. The exposed steel of the bridge and ducts and plywood floor in the loft create the desired industrial feel. Photo shows bridge railing before clear-glass panels were installed. Photo taken at D on floor on floor plan.

and bridge lead to the second floor, where clear-finished plywood serves as flooring (see photo above). Exposed, galvanized spiral duct and exhaust fans continue the loft aesthetic. For privacy in the master bedroom, Mike installed tempered, obscure-glass panels below the railing.

Designing a space-efficient, open-plan home requires careful attention to detail. The kitchen cabinetry reaches the ceiling, and base cabinets are accessible on both sides of the kitchen counter. To conserve space, Mike asked to have the master tub and shower considered as one room with a drain (see photo top facing page). A tankless water heater that serves the whole house fits between two studs. In the master suite, the washer and dryer sit between the master bath and the walk-in closet to keep laundry corralled.

Richard Wintersole is an architect in Fort Worth, Texas. A member of AIA, his projects have been featured in local and national publications.

A House Disguised as a Cottage

I doubt many people arrive at their country estates these days in horse-drawn carriages. As a result, an architect might pass an entire career without ever getting a chance to design a traditional gate-house. But at the turn of the century, these cottagelike buildings could be found marking the approach to many a large country house. An arched passageway through the center of the building was high enough so that a carriage driver could deliver his passengers without getting his hat knocked off. Outdated as it might be from a practical point of view, this architectural style has a special charm—and it was exactly what my clients were looking for.

ABOVE AND FACING PAGE   House with a hole. This gate-house-style home has a passageway leading to a private backyard. Photo (facing page) taken at A on floor plan. Photo (above) taken at B on floor plan.

While Mark and Karen Prentiss wanted something unique, they also hoped their new house would fit comfortably in a neighborhood of well-crafted, turn-of-the-century houses that include small Victorians, Greek revivals, bungalows, and Cape Cod houses. A gatehouse design that looked as if it had been around in the 1920s, they thought, would be a good fit with the mixed New England architecture of Woods Hole, Massachusetts. Although the idea of a cottage appealed to them, the interior spaces they had in mind added up to a full-fledged house. Who better to balance these competing interests, they asked, than an architect who had grown up right in town?

I was taken right away with the prospect of designing a house with a hole in the middle (see photo pp. 68, 69). I imagined an archway that would provide glimpses from the street into a level, quiet area at the back of the house. To accommodate the Prentisses' desire that the house not be too imposing, I used a few tricks that make it appear shorter and smaller than it really is. It may look something like a cottage on the outside, but inside are the 8-ft. 4-in. ceilings and open spaces of an ample house.

To Fit with Its Neighbors, the House Needed Familiar Details

To get something as unique as a gatehouse to fit in with the more typical types of houses already on the block, I used similar building shapes and detailing, and oriented the house so that it faced the street, just as other houses in the neighborhood do. Houses on the block typically include gable ends of 24 ft. or so, roof pitches of 12-in-12, and generous roof overhangs. In addition to using these features, I also borrowed some specific details from nearby houses: a five-panel door style and crown-molding profiles, a garage-door style from up the road, and a trim detail in which the head casings extend well past the side casings.

Then, to make a pleasing composition of house shapes, I mixed small, medium, and large elements. There are small details, such as ½-in.-wide window muntins and 5-in. trim and shingle coursing, that give way to medium-size shapes, such as the 5-ft.-wide front porch, and eventually to large shapes: the 16-ft.-dia., two-story tower, the 24-ft. gable end at the garage, and the 50-ft. side of the house facing the street.

A simple way to give one-story, cottage-like houses more room is to poke dormers from the roof. They can provide lots of second-floor space. But as the floor area of the second floor approaches that of the first floor, this approach becomes less convincing. By locating a large shed dormer and a second-story bedroom on the back of the house, where they are not visible from the street, I hoped to preserve the look of a small house out front.

A Steep Roof and Exterior Detailing Give the House Its Personality

A dominant roof and dormers, plus the trim that helps to define their shapes, are vital visual ingredients on the street side of the house. The 12-in-12 pitch of the main roof helps to give it mass, and the three sizes of gables add variety. The two dormers near the top of the roof are small, and they use triangular sash instead of a more traditional rectangular shape. Still, they are an attractive source of light inside (see photo top facing page). The varying sizes of two other gables on the front of the house—a slightly larger version over the entry and a much larger gable over the archway—are complementary without being redundant.

LEFT **Small but effective.** A tri-angular dormer in the master bed-room is not obtrusively large from the outside, but it's large enough to cast a pleasing afternoon light. Photo taken at H on floor plan.

LEFT **A high ceiling makes the library seem light and airy.** The 16-ft. ceiling in the second floor of the tower is unencumbered by collar ties, thanks to a triple top plate that forms a tension ring and prevents the walls from spreading. Photo taken at G on floor plan.

When it came to the tower's roof, a 12-in-12 pitch would have looked squat, so I flared the lower part of the roof with a gentle curve and increased the pitch on the upper roof to 14-in-12. Inside the tower on the second floor is a library with a 16-ft. ceiling (see photo above). I was able to avoid the use of collar ties, leaving the space open, by tripling the tower's top plate and bolting the overlapping ends together to create a tension ring. Plywood sheathing on the roof and walls also helps to prevent the walls from spreading.

Library

Bedroom

G

Dn

Open to below

I

Up

F

Up

H

Master bedroom

Second floor

A HOUSE BUILT AROUND A PRIVATE OUTDOOR SPACE

An archway between the garage and the house leads to a backyard sheltered on one side by the house and on the other by a terraced bank. A roomy kitchen and a cathedral-ceilinged living room both front this protected area, with access through French doors in the living room.

SPECS

BEDROOMS: **2**

BATHROOMS: **2½**

SIZE: **2,320 sq. ft.**

COST: **$145.00 per sq. ft.**

COMPLETED: **1998**

LOCATION: **Woods Hole, Massachusetts**

ARCHITECT: **William F. Rolansky**

BUILDERS: **Peter Ochs, Doug Brown**

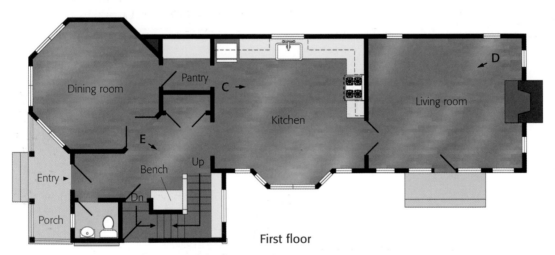

Dining room

Pantry

C

Living room

D

Kitchen

E

Bench

Up

Entry

Porch

Dn

First floor

Archway

B

North

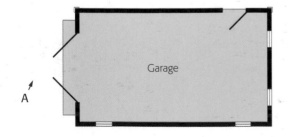

Garage

A

0 2 4   8 ft.

Photos taken at lettered positions.

Although roof rafters are 2x12s, rafter tails are ripped down to 5½ in. where they cross the wall line. That keeps the fascia from looking too heavy. And by leaving the rafter tails square, rather than ending them in a plumb cut, the builders were able to use the same profile crown molding on the rakes and the eaves. These important trim details outside, however, would not have come off as well without the seasoned crew of boat-builders on the general contractor's payroll. These talented individuals were masters at generating fair curves on rogue timbers, and evidence of the crew's skill is especially visible in the trusses over the archway leading to the backyard.

I usually advocate asphalt shingles because they last just about as long as cedar, are less of a fire hazard, and are much less expensive. But here, western red-cedar roof shingles complement the rest of the house perfectly. They are nailed over Cedar Breather from Benjamin Obdyke Inc. (see Sources p. 75), a nylon mesh installed between the shingles and the felt roof underlayment. Cedar Breather is designed to allow the backside of the shingles to dry out, preventing moisture from accumulating between sheathing and shingle. Although the material is a bit expensive, it should increase the life span of the wood roof, balancing out the added cost while helping to save a precious forest resource.

A Simple Floor Plan Makes the Most of a Private Outdoor Space

Inside spaces, especially on the first floor, are open, light, and airy. The archway between the house and the garage creates a long wing perpendicular to the street where a dining room, kitchen, pantry, and living room are located essentially in line (see floor plans facing page). A bay window in the roomy kitchen (see photo below) and French doors in the living room (see photo top p. 74) face the enclosed backyard. The

Kitchen has a period flavor. Oak cabinets stained a nut brown are reminiscent of a Craftsman-era interior. White brick-laid tiles and a period light fixture also are suggestive of the early 20th century. Photo taken at C on floor plan.

Although the interior is not elaborate, details such as a bullnose molding cap on a window and door casings, hardwood floors, and custom stairs are aimed at making the space appealing.

ABOVE Easy access to the backyard. French doors in the living room make it easy to get to a protected, terraced backyard. Photo taken at D on floor plan.

ABOVE Up and over. Access to the master bedroom is across a short hall concealed in the trusses of the archway. The door on the left opens to the master bathroom. Photo taken at I on floor plan.

view is tranquil. Big rocks form a two-tier retaining wall on steep banking where flowers have been planted. Although the space feels private, there still are views through the archway toward the street.

The archway created some interesting problems on the second floor. With the master bedroom over the garage, access is over the top of the archway. That means going up three steps, down a short hall, and then down three steps (see photo left). The master bathroom is off the hall. A skylight facing the back of the house brings in natural light (see photo top facing page) while fixtures and the beadboard wainscoting were chosen to enhance the 1920s flavor of the house.

There is only one other bedroom on the second floor, occupying the space over the

ABOVE Trim details set this staircase apart. Both riser and tread appear to wrap around the corner of these stairs. Limiting materials to clear-finished oak and white-painted surfaces sharpens the effect. Photo taken at E on floor plan.

LEFT A small bathroom can still be inviting. Illuminated by a skylight, the master bath makes the most of a small space. Light-colored paint and white wainscoting keep the room from feeling cramped. Photo taken at F on floor plan.

kitchen. But the library could be converted to a bedroom if the need ever arose. The library has 360 degrees of continuous shelving, and the built-in drawers could be used as dressers. A ring of rope lighting above the bookcases provides a source of indirect light.

Although the interior is not elaborate, details such as a bullnose molding cap on window and door casings, hardwood floors, and custom stairs are aimed at making the space appealing. One of the touches I like is the small bench at the bottom of the stairs that looks like an extension of the oak stair treads (see photo top right).

William F. Roslansky, an avid windsurfer and furniture maker, is an architect in Woods Hole, Massachusetts.

SOURCES

Benjamin Obdyke Incorporated
199 Precision Drive
Horsham, PA 19044
(800) 346-7655
www.obdyke.com

One of the obvious advantages of cohousing.
With cars restricted to the perimeter, children are free
to play in spaces that look and feel both public and
private.

A Deliberate Neighborhood

ARVEY ARDEN, WHO EDITED THE WRITINGS OF NATIVE American activist Leonard Peltier and wrote the book *Wisdomkeepers*, once visited a Lakota tribal elder who had no telephone. Arden knocked on the door, and when it opened, he said to the old man who answered, "Hi, I'm Harvey Arden." The Native elder said, "Come on in. I know why you're here. You white folks lost all your instructions, and you've come to get ours." Cohousing is a new set of ideas for making good neighborhoods in a culture that has lost its instructions and values about housing.

Like many beautiful places, Martha's Vineyard has a serious affordable-housing crisis. Our problems are not unique, but they are intensified by a wildly inflated real-estate market and fixed boundaries. As my colleague Derrill Bazzy says, "There's no down-the-road on an island." The shortage of good housing for residents of moderate income endangers the island's diversity, charm, social health, and economic prosperity. We've done well with the preservation of open space, but solving the affordable housing crisis is like trying to turn around an ocean liner in a sea of molasses. Far too often, *development* has been an ugly word and has had unfortunate results. But that doesn't have to be the case. When you think about development, ask the following question first: Are you proposing to invent something that the community needs? If not, why bother? Martha's Vineyard needs high-quality affordable housing for working people, but other community needs are also linked to this issue:

- Open space preserved in perpetuity.
- Restoration of agricultural land.
- Areas for businesses to locate where they will not contribute to strip development.
- Community systems for converting human waste to nutrients so that it doesn't foul our one and only aquifer.
- Neighborhoods that encourage a high level of social interaction.

ALL HOUSES START WITH THE SAME BASIC PLAN

One way to help keep down costs was to limit customization of the homes. Therefore, all 16 houses are variations on the same basic two-bedroom plan. Options included a third bedroom and a second bath, a fourth bedroom, and various bump-outs. The two plans below show the range from most basic (see drawings left) to most complex (see drawings right).

Two-bedroom plan
(1,094 sq. ft.)

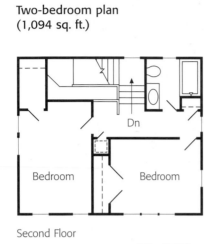

Second Floor

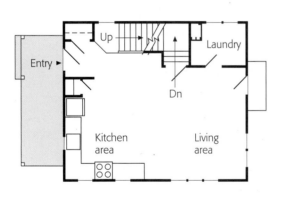

First Floor

Four-bedroom plan
(1,788 sq. ft.)

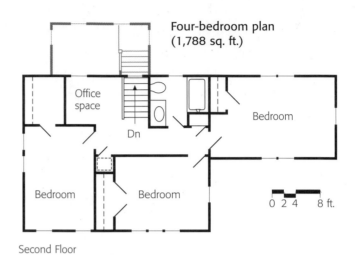

Second Floor

First Floor

What Is Cohousing?

Cohousing, a Danish housing concept developed in the 1970s, may be a way to satisfy all these needs at once. Cohousing communities are neighborhoods of 12 to 35 homes. Houses are tightly clustered, and cars are relegated to the perimeter. There are extensive community facilities, usually anchored by a common house where residents share a few meals a week, where guests can stay, and where a variety of activities takes place. The common house is not only a community hub; it also provides residents with space not needed on a daily basis, thereby allowing individual homes to be smaller. Another fundamental principle of cohousing is that the residents of a new project are the developers. They make decisions—such as size, spacing, and number of houses—as a group, and the process of doing so creates community bonds.

Some years ago, during a talk about Vineyard housing, I suggested the potential of cohousing. Two couples approached me afterward and said, "This is just what we need here. Why aren't we doing it?" I replied, "I've just been waiting for a few people like you. Let's go." That was the beginning of Island Cohousing, and soon after, a core group of households hired our design/build company, South Mountain, to conduct a land search, to facilitate development of the group, and then to design and build a deliberate neighborhood (see photo p. 76).

Working with, Not against, the Land-Use Boards Was Key

By the time we started shopping for land, two important things had changed: One, my family and I joined the group; and two, the employee/owners of South Mountain decided the same thing—that we would move the company there (see drawings pp. 80, 81). We found a 50-acre piece of woodland in West Tisbury, bought it, divided it into several pieces (one for the business, which shared the cost), and soon had a 30-acre parcel for the cohousing community at relatively low cost.

Unfortunately, our project violated current zoning in 10 different ways. The area was zoned for a maximum density of one house per 3 acres, for instance, and it was also zoned residential. Friends in local politics said, "Nice idea. You'll never do it here."

But we carried the collaborative methods we've developed in our business into the public arena. Our regional planning agency, the Martha's Vineyard Commission, has

Carts Transport Goods

Carts go where cars can't. Because cars are kept on the perimeter, community-owned garden carts are used to ferry groceries from car to house.

When we first considered moving to Island Cohousing, I worried about the carts (see photo above). Wouldn't I hate not being able to park next to my house and having to haul stuff in a silly garden cart instead? I was used to unloading things easily, including my sleeping toddler, from my driveway to the house. Proximity to the cars even influenced the house we selected. But now that I'm here, it no longer feels like an issue. Kids outgrow naps, and little ones can be carried (car seat and all) comfortably in the cart.

The carts hold more than you can carry, so you can move groceries, purse, backpacks, jackets, beach towels and chairs, empty food containers, and school art projects all in one trip—way easier than back and forth from car to door with armloads of stuff.

When it rains, it's no different than going from the grocery store to your car: You move fast. And if something is especially big, heavy, or fragile, we allow ourselves to drop the ropes and pull our carts up to the house to drop it off.

Ultimately, the joy of watching the kids safely run free, ride bikes, and play ball is worth a soggy paper bag any day.

Julia Kidd lives with her husband, son, and dog in house No. 13 at Island Cohousing.

South Mountain Moves In

After 15 years, we needed far more space for our offices, shop, and especially storage. Because we build primarily with recycled lumber, we need lots of space to stockpile old beams, boards, and planks (see photo below). By joining forces with the cohousing development, we were able to buy a larger piece of land and develop it together, thereby saving on land and infrastructure costs. Being close to such a neighborhood allows some people who live in the cohousing community and work at South Mountain to walk to work. Mixing small neighborhoods and low-impact, responsive businesses, a common rural pattern in the past, is healthier than strip-development and industrial-park models. —J. A.

ABOVE New headquarters. South Mountain Company occupies land next to the cohousing project.

COHOUSING: A BETTER KIND OF DEVELOPMENT

Modeled after a Danish concept, Island Cohousing on Martha's Vineyard features 16 houses tightly clustered around a pedestrian commons. Residents acted as their own developers to design the kind of community they wanted to live in. Cars are relegated to the perimeter. Facilities such as the common house, the pond, and the gardens are shared by all residents.

South Mountain Company

Island Cohousing began with the purchase of a 50-acre woodland. Several lots were sold off to help reduce costs, which left 7 acres for South Mountain Company and 30 acres for the 16-house development.

broad regulatory powers. Our project had to go before the panel as a development of regional impact. The commission's job is to determine whether proposed projects will be more beneficial than detrimental to the community. Most developers see commission members as adversaries. We saw their purpose as being the same as ours: to shape a better community. So we came to them with a project that anticipated their concerns. Instead of regulating, they were able to work with us to create a better project (see sidebar p. 82). When the commission-

ers finally voted approval, they issued a decision with 15 conditions. All of them began with the words, "We accept the applicant's offer to …"

We had a green light to build 16 new houses with a variety of common facilities. Tight clustering would let us keep 85% of the 30-acre parcel in open space. A strong environmental program would influence the design and construction of both site and houses.

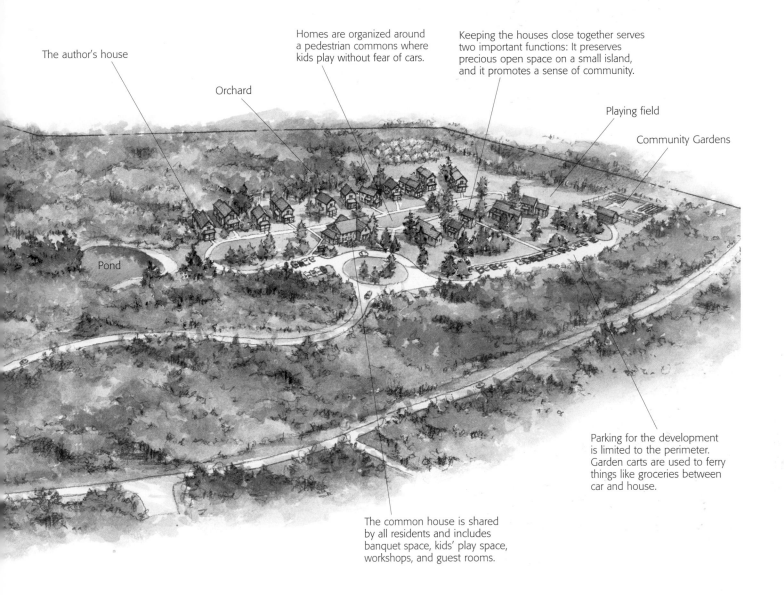

The author's house

Orchard

Homes are organized around a pedestrian commons where kids play without fear of cars.

Keeping the houses close together serves two important functions: It preserves precious open space on a small island, and it promotes a sense of community.

Playing field

Community Gardens

Pond

Parking for the development is limited to the perimeter. Garden carts are used to ferry things like groceries between car and house.

The common house is shared by all residents and includes banquet space, kids' play space, workshops, and guest rooms.

Keeping Costs Down Wasn't Easy

The core group of homeowners, which by this time represented 10 households, was committed to accommodating income diversity and providing desperately needed affordable housing. Therefore, we agreed that four houses would be deeply subsidized and sold to qualifying buyers who made less than 80% of median local income. Four more houses would be lightly subsidized to accommodate those for whom Vineyard

housing prices are just out of reach. Here's how we subsidized the houses:

- Internal price structuring, which shifted a higher percentage of the shared costs (development and design costs, infrastructure, and common facilities) to the larger houses. In other words, those of us who bought the three- and four-bedroom homes not only paid additional construction costs but also paid a higher percentage of the shared costs for the project.

Zoning Laws Can Change

Because the Island Cohousing project violated local zoning in many ways, we had to use a difficult, cumbersome method (a Massachusetts law known as the "anti-snob-zoning law") to get through the regulatory process. But the town boards all thought this kind of project was precisely the type of development needed, and it caused people to ask the question, "Why won't our zoning permit this?" Soon the planning board hired a consultant and enlisted the help of residents to do a comprehensive rewrite of town zoning, to create a document that would encourage the kind of development and housing we need and want without opening the floodgates to overdevelopment. Tricky task. Last year, the new zoning rules, which contain a number of innovative affordable-housing initiatives and incentives, were passed at the town meeting. Today, a similar project could be built without violating zoning. —J. A.

A strong environmental program would influence the design and construction of both sites and houses.

- Cash fund-raising (tax-deductible donations to the Island Affordable Housing Fund).
- Reduced mortgage rates from our two public-spirited banks (6% as opposed to 8%).

The four deeply subsidized houses also have limited-equity deed restrictions designed to maintain perpetual affordability by limiting appreciation and future resale prices. The two-bedroom homes appraised for about $200,000. We sold four of them for about $120,000 and wrote into their deeds that they must always sell for 60% of their appraised value. (Remember that this is Martha's Vineyard: A new house for $120,000 is *very* affordable here.)

Additionally, we used a variety of means to keep down the costs of all the houses.

- Production-building methods, repetitive design, and minimal customization.
- South Mountain sharing infrastructure costs such as roads and power.
- Selling several building lots from the remaining 20 acres to reduce land costs.
- Reduced rates for South Mountain's design and construction services.

The last one needs explanation. We found a way we could reduce our rates dramatically without a detrimental effect on our company's bottom line. If we build a $1 million house and charge 20% overhead and profit (which we do), we receive $200,000. Island Cohousing was a $4 million project. If we could commit the same amount of our limited human resources to this project as to the building of a million-dollar house, we could charge 5% overhead and profit, and come out at the same place. So we planned to provide full-time construction management and supervision services, but our crews would do little of the actual work (they would be out making money on that million-dollar house). This approach was marginally successful; we had to commit more resources than we had intended.

Weighing Environmental Costs against Pocketbook Costs

We suggested to the group that some of the green-building approaches that South Mountain uses in all its projects (like finishing our houses, inside and out, with salvaged and certified lumber, first-rate energy efficiency, extensive use of recycled materials) wouldn't be too expensive. Others would. For example, we could generate our power with wind and photovoltaics to be a net energy producer. We could do a district heating system (one heating plant supplying all the homes) fueled by the wood that grows each year on our land. We could convert our human waste into valuable nutrients by using composting toilets.

Photovoltaic and wind-generated power proved to be too expensive and could be done later (we committed to 300 sq. ft. of uninterrupted south-facing roof on each house and marked a site for a wind turbine). The second idea was not feasible

ABOVE Homes nestled in the trees. Construction would have been simpler if all the trees had been cut down, but working around them resulted in new homes that look like an old neighborhood.

Living with a Composting Toilet

No, a composting toilet doesn't smell bad (see photo right). You pretty much use it like a conventional toilet, except you don't have to flush, which means it's quieter. About once a week, you need to throw in some cedar shavings. Composting toilets are a bit harder to clean; there isn't a toilet bowl filled with water to make cleaning easier.

Each composting toilet (Clivus Multrum U.S.A.) sits over an 18-in. chute that leads to a fiberglass chamber in the basement. Maintenance includes opening the chamber once a month and leveling the pile, emptying liquid fertilizer every six months, and emptying compost every two years. A paid community member ensures that the toilets are properly maintained.

Paul Lazes lives with his wife, son, and dog in house No. 13 at Island Cohousing.

ABOVE They don't look that different. To protect the aquifer on Martha's Vineyard, all the homes in the cohousing project have composting toilets.

because the group was unwilling to commit to tight-enough house spacing. The third had an interesting result.

Martha's Vineyard's aquifer can be easily polluted. The cohousing group took this fact to heart and decided to equip the houses with composting toilets (see sidebar p. 83): a large expense, a lifestyle change and a risk. Will people want these houses, will banks finance them, will appraisers value them, will the town allow them? These questions all turned out to have positive answers.

Another essential environmental commitment was to save the trees on the site. For ease of construction, most developments in wooded areas begin by clearing the site. Instead, we mapped and marked the best trees. We sited our houses based on this mapping and protected the trees during construction. This complication probably cost about $100,000, but what kind of landscape replacement could we have bought for $100,000? Very little. Today, the houses nestle comfortably in those trees (see photo top p. 83).

Deciding Who Lives Where

The group was the client; it was South Mountain's job to serve their needs, which in this case took us beyond the traditional roles of developer, architect, and builder. We also needed to facilitate group development, teaching people to become an effective decision-making organization.

This process changed perceptions in remarkable ways. Tight clustering of the houses was a goal. We used an old island neighborhood, the campgrounds at Oak Bluffs, as a model and studied it as a group, learning about the effects of house spacing, siting devices, and community patterns. I recall walking back to the car after our first session there. One group member walking with me said that it's lucky we had such a

large piece of property because she would never consider living in a house closer than 100 ft. to a neighboring house. My heart sank at the time, but today, she is delighted to live 20 ft. away from the neighboring house.

Along with the trees (and good solar access), the siting of the houses on the property considered a matrix of proximities (see painting p. 81): distance from parking; distance from the common house; distance from pond setbacks; distance from the main path; distance to end house or middle house; etc. Slightly higher values were assigned to those sites with clear benefits (end sites with direct views to the pond or the agricultural area, for instance). But how

would we determine who got which housing site?

The group met around a large site map with the 5,000-sq.-ft. lots laid out. Each household had a blue dot (first choice) and a red dot (second choice). We placed our dots. There were enough differences that the dots were well distributed. Some people wanted to be close to parking. Some wanted automobiles to be as far away as possible. Some wanted to be close to the common house. Some wanted more privacy. Some were willing to pay for views; some were not. There were only a few conflicting interests.

The two or more households that wanted the same lot then met to see if anyone had a more serious reason for wanting a particular lot. This discussion was all it took. Within a few hours, everyone had either their first or second choice. Siting diversity was the key to this success.

One Floor Plan, Few Options

Customization has often been the virus that infects the cohousing process and brings it down. It's impossible to achieve low-cost, high-quality and custom homes simultaneously for all. If this fact is not understood, costs can spiral out of control.

In this regard, we had the good fortune to benefit from the experiences of other co-

A few options on the interior. All the homes feature a kitchen that's open directly to the living area. Options included hardwood cabinets, slate counters, and a first-floor bedroom at the back of the house.

> *Architecturally, Island Cohousing is less about the houses and more about the spaces between them.*

housing projects. Not that our group had different inclinations; everyone wanted custom homes. But our design process limited customization while making room for individual desires. Our basic house design is a simple 22-ft. by 26-ft. two-story rectangle with a full cellar (see floor plans p. 78). The public areas are on the first level (see photo p. 85) and there are two bedrooms and a bath on the second. Options included a third bedroom and a second bath, a fourth bedroom, and several bump-outs. All the additions derive from the same basic plan, and the smaller houses are designed so that the additions can be made easily later.

The group was self-disciplined and able to agree on most choices, right down to the tile selections and interior paint colors. A critically important tool was the six-page design objectives we had compiled and adopted early on, which spelled out our commitments regarding design, environment, economy, and community. We often referred to it for guidance during the design process.

Don't get me wrong; we veered from the path often. For example, there was a time when group members wanted the houses to be shorter, have more interesting shapes, and have upstairs interior space created by dormers. This plan would have violated two of our design commitments: One, the forms should be simple, spare, and straightforward; and two, we should plan for the use of solar hot water or photovoltaic panels, and therefore provide at least 300 sq. ft. of contiguous, unobstructed south-facing roof at 40 degrees or more on each dwelling. We were rigorous about refocusing discussions so that we wouldn't wreak havoc with schedule, budget, or design.

The Community Begins Well before the Construction Finishes

There was a gradual shift from concern about individual interests to the interests of the community as a whole. Members realized that the basic shaping of community must happen first, whereas they can shape their own homes and adjacent landscapes by adding personal touches over time. A hinge point in this transformative process came when we considered the house exteriors.

We provided several exterior options that, along with the different sizes and configurations, would help to break up the sameness: different porch roofs, a small selection of roof and window colors, and optional gable-end wall detailing. When considering these choices, someone said, "There's no way I could ever have that dark-green color on my house." Someone else said, "To tell you the truth, I don't care that much what I've got on my house. I'm more concerned about what you've got on your house. That's what I'll be looking at." And the group quickly agreed that we, as the designers, should take personal preferences loosely into account but should plan a pattern that would make a well-designed community. At that moment, it was clear that the process had created an excellent group of decision-makers.

Architecturally, Island Cohousing is less about the houses and more about the spaces between them. In plan, it's like houses on a street facing each other, except that instead of a street, a pedestrian commons separates the buildings.

Residents make decisions—such as size, spacing, and number of houses—as a group, and the process of doing so creates community bonds.

A community breakfast. Four months after moving in, the neighborhood got together on the commons to serve pancakes for the 20 resident kids on the first day of school.

It's Really about the Kids

The first year of living here has been extraordinary. There are 20 kids, and they are surely the defining image and the driving force. For example, on the first day of school, all the kids gathered at 7 A.M. at the picnic tables under the oaks. A group of parents prepared a huge pancake breakfast (see photo above). The kids ate their fill and headed off for the bus stop.

The mistakes we made and the lessons we learned could fill another article. After the project was complete, we compiled a list of lessons learned in three areas: business, design, and construction. Here's an example from each:

1. Change orders and options. There were too many judgment calls and too much jockeying. We had a good understanding with the group, but we should have created a written policy, obtained approval from the group, and stuck to it rigorously. In this arena, informality brings chaos.

2. The entry is the biggest design failure in the houses. It's too small; there should have been a real mudroom. Minor improvement and expansion would make a big difference.

3. Our waste program was insufficient. Therefore, we went over budget on waste disposal and did not meet environmental goals. We needed a better system and a clearer understanding with subcontractors about responsibility and handling of waste.

Would we do it again? We would, and we will. This collaboration was first rate, with tremendously satisfying results, but I'd hate to leave it at that. After all, how could we spend three years screwing up daily and not practice what we learned by doing similar projects in the future?

John Abrams is president of South Mountain Company, an employee-owned design/build firm in West Tisbury, Massachusetts, that specializes in ecologically sensitive dwellings and neighborhoods.

SOURCES

Clivus Multrum Incorporated
15 Union Street
Lawrence, MA 01840
(800) 425-4887

South Mountain Co., Inc.
Red Arrow Rd.
West Tisbury, MA 02575
www.southmountain.com

A House with Wings

THE DESIGN PROCESS IS AS OFTEN ABOUT SURPRISE AS IT IS about deliberation. After spending a year in Japan, Jill Kleinberg developed a real appreciation for the sukiya tradition of the Japanese farmhouse. Among other things, this style emphasizes plain materials and a sense that house and garden are intertwined. When Jill asked us to design her new house here in Kansas, she pointed us in the direction of

The storm shrine. A rooftop observation booth is the perfect place to watch the summer sky. Photo taken at A on floor plan.

this traditional architecture. After months of design studies, David Sain (my associate) and I came up with a design. When Jill saw the first model, she thought that it looked like a tombo, the Japanese word for *dragonfly*. We were surprised by the association; we hadn't seen it, but the name stuck.

Like many of our clients, Jill was long on ideas but short on funds to put them together. We designed and built this house and developed the site for

Living area benefits from light.
Large south-facing windows brighten the front of the house. Ceiling light fixtures above the translucent panels augment the sunlight. Photo taken at B on floor plan.

$200,000. Backing out the costs for driveway, septic, water, and garage, we were left with only a little more than $150,000 to build the house. Working with less than $75 per sq. ft., we had to find simple materials and an equally simple plan to make it work. It took four of us about nine months to build this house (not including nearly six months of part-time design); during that

time, we hired only one subcontractor, who handled the HVAC.

The house (see photo pp. 88–89) is made of two distinct parts: a wide front section that's topped with a winglike roof and a rear section oriented at right angles to the front. Three parallel concrete walls (see sidebar p. 95) make up the single-story front section, which contains the kitchen, the study, and the living/dining room; the

with a stand of oak trees. We placed the house facing south to bring in as much light as possible.

We created a reflecting pool at the front of the house that ties in with the concrete deck. Extending the design to the landscape helps to increase the house's sense of openness. The pool adds a bright spot to the living area (see photo facing page). As the sun moves through the southern sky, it is often reflected as shimmering light onto the walls and ceiling. The dancing light also works to draw the eye outside.

Details in Concrete and Steel

Once the concrete walls were standing, we began framing the wood walls inside; I left an airspace of nearly an inch between the insulated stud walls and the uninsulated concrete. Recycled form plywood became the roof deck, which we covered with a rubber membrane. The exterior complete, we could install many of the cabinets and other details that kept us busy in the shop all winter when the weather was too nasty to work outside.

After applying a skim coat of plaster to the walls, we set the simple birch-plywood cabinets and the concrete countertops. We stick-framed the big walk-in pantry for the kitchen (see photo top p. 92) and the closet for the study. Their exterior walls create a transition between the front and back sections of the house (see floor plans p. 94).

We made liberal use of 13-ga. square steel tubing finished in black enamel paint. In the master bath, we used tube stock to make a frame for the mirror and an enclosure for the shower. Steel tubing also turns up as frames for the overhangs that shelter the exterior doors, as the bowstring trusses in the screened porch and as the armature for the revolving door that leads from the

Incandescent lamps above the fiberglass panels cast a warm, ambient glow over the room.

wedge-shaped back portion has a wooden second story that emerges from the first-story base of concrete walls and contains the bedrooms and bathrooms.

One of the reasons this remote site was so attractive to us was that we could take maximum advantage of its gently sloping landscape. The house is nestled against a south-facing hill and looks out over an open area bordered by a small creek lined

RIGHT Kitchen benefits from clean lines of simple fixtures. Birch-plywood cabinets were inexpensive and add a note of warmth to a room with concrete detailing. Photo taken at D on floor plan.

BELOW A cool and breezy refuge. The screened porch is off the east side of the living room. Photo taken at C on floor plan.

Extending the design to the landscape helps to increase the house's sense of openness.

master bedroom to the rooftop walkway and Jill's storm shrine. Wrapped in stainless steel scrounged from a local scrap yard, the shrine is the perfect place to watch summer storms churn into view.

In addition to the precast concrete tub (see photo facing page), we also made concrete countertops and bathroom wall tiles. We cast the counters and tiles face down in plywood forms with no form release.

Instead, we spray-painted a sea-green enamel from a can onto the form. When the concrete was poured in, the paint bled into the finish and gave us the subtle effect we wanted.

The mix consisted of 1 part portland cement, 2 parts sand, and 4 parts pea gravel (no bigger than ¼ in.). Reinforcing the concrete with a frame of ⅜-in. rebar, we also added some short polypropylene fibers as insurance against cracking. We used the same fibers in the wall tiles, which are 2 ft. sq. by 1½ in. thick. But we decided to forgo the steel reinforcing in these thin pieces. The tiles are held in place by lag screws run through holes in the tiles made during the casting process.

We set the tiles after pouring a full slab in the bathroom for the finish floor. Mixing the concrete on site gave me time to slope the shower floor correctly to its drain and to get a nice finish on the entire area. A rubber membrane beneath the slab flows into the floor drain as a backup.

Fiberglass Panels: A New Use for a Common Material

Throughout Jill's house, corrugated-fiberglass panels turn up in some unusual places.

Concrete tub is focus of the bath. The tub is sealed with epoxy pool paint. Cast-concrete wall tiles and welded towel racks keep lines spare. Photo taken at E on floor plan.

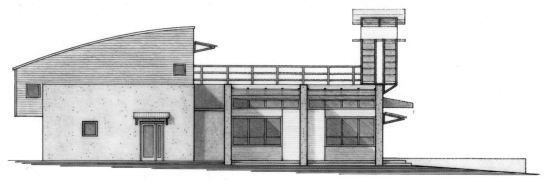

FRESH DESIGN, FAMILIAR MATERIALS

This open plan provides ample flow between each of the four public areas: living room, dining room, kitchen, and study. These rooms are shaped by the three parallel concrete walls at the front of the house and include various spaces as they meet the outdoors. The study and kitchen include walk-in storage areas that are recessed in the walls. The less public area in the dovetail-shaped rear includes the guest room, the bath, and the utility room. The upper level contains an open master bedroom, a walk-in dressing area, a large open bathing area, and the steps to the walkway and storm shrine.

SPECS

BEDROOMS: 2

BATHROOMS: 2

SIZE: 2,100 sq. ft.

COST: $75.00 per sq. ft., excluding site costs, sewer, water, and garage

COMPLETED: 2000

LOCATION: Lawrence, Kansas

ARCHITECT/BUILDER: Rockhill and Associates

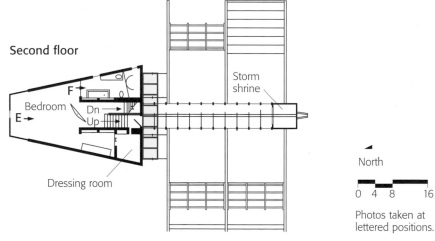

Second floor

F

Bedroom

Dn

E → Up

Dressing room

Storm shrine

North

0 4 8   16 ft.

Photos taken at lettered positions.

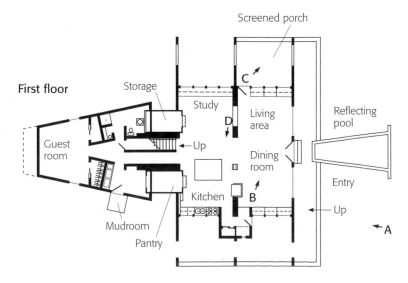

Screened porch

First floor

Storage

Study

C

Living area

D

Guest room

Up

Dining room

Reflecting pool

B

Kitchen

Entry

Up

A

Mudroom

Pantry

ABOVE The secluded bedroom area opens to the roof. At the house's rear, the bedroom includes a bath, a walk-in closet and stairs to the roof. Photo taken at F on floor plan.

This material is typically used for translucent roofs on outbuildings or over a patio. At 75¢ per sq. ft., it's inexpensive, and it goes up in a hurry. We used two types on this project: translucent white and semitransparent clear. We applied the white variety to the living-room ceiling, where it acts as a room-size light fixture. Incandescent lamps above the fiberglass panels cast a warm, ambient glow over the room.

We used the clear, semitransparent fiberglass panels for other offbeat purposes, especially in the master bath (see photo above). Next to the tub, horizontal panels create a sleek wall that lets in light from the stairwell to the roof. Hung vertically, more panels form a cylinder-shaped shower stall.

We liked the veil of transparency the panels gave the bath without the solidity of opaque walls. From inside, it looks beautiful, emitting shades of magenta and cyan when light is reflected in the right way.

Dan Rockhill is an architect, a builder, and a professor of architecture at the University of Kansas. The work of Rockhill and Associates can be seen at www.Rockhillandassociates.com.

Pouring Freestanding Concrete

The predominant material in the house is concrete: It's strong, it's economical, and we like working with it. Although concrete walls enclose both sections of the house, we were preoccupied with the three freestanding concrete walls in front and with the dovetail in the back. To create the 8-in.-thick, 16-ft.-high walls, we needed to form and pour each wall in two 8-ft.-tall sections, one atop the other (see top photo below). A monolithic pour was out of the question; the pressure exerted on a form of that height would blow apart the form.

We built our own forms from plywood and 2x4s and recycled the materials back into the house with little waste. We built block-outs for the large openings and took great pains to cross-brace the forms with 2x4s (see bottom photo below) to resist pressure. We also braced the corners, but a form still blew out on the second lift. There's nothing that can come close to the sound of 5 yards of concrete swooshing out of a form and the sinking feeling it produces. Having to solve the problem quickly can be a little disconcerting. On a windy 95°F day in Kansas, you have about 20 minutes to make repairs after you shut down the pump before the concrete sets up in the hose and you have to buy a new pump. After repairing the damage, we finished pouring the walls. —D. R.

LEFT High walls are poured in stages. To prevent excess pressure from building and blowing out forms, the walls were cast in two 8-ft. sections.

LEFT Freestanding walls are braced carefully. After the forms had been stripped, the 16-ft.-high walls were temporarily reinforced with 2x4s.

Modern Living in a New England Village

ONE OF THE GREAT EXPERIENCES OF MY LIFE WAS LIVING IN a New York City loft with 13-ft. ceilings. Day after day, sunlight poured in, creating a beautiful living and working environment. Years later, I moved to Maine and bought a 125-year-old traditional house in the center of Yarmouth village. Although the house was beautiful outside, the inside was just a series of small boxlike rooms. Getting from one room to the next required going through two doorways and crossing a central-stair hall. I loved village life but longed for the spacious feeling of the city loft. I resolved someday to find a way to unite these two apparent opposites in a house of my own design.

Rear walls become picture frames. Windows and doors in the rear (photo taken at B on floor plan) create a connection between indoors and outdoors.

ABOVE A lack of windows in front creates privacy. Photo taken at A on floor plan.

From the street the modern quality and lines of the house are subtle.

ABOVE **A great place to hang out.** An open front porch complete with a white-cedar deck, a fir-paneled ceiling, and turned-pine columns provides a great place to relax and a transition from indoors to outdoors. Photo taken at G on floor plan.

It Began with a Simple Gable

While walking on a back road in Yarmouth one day, I noticed a small for-sale sign hidden in the woods between two traditional farmhouses. Several phone calls later, a 1-acre lot was mine. I spent a lot of time walking the wooded site and studying the surrounding neighborhood. Simple gabled roofs are everywhere in Maine; they line up along our streets and remind me of weathered fishermen's square jaws jutting defiantly into the wind. I decided to use this simplest of building forms as the starting point for the house.

The main house and the garage roofs are simple gables with long, low sloping roofs to one side, like a shed on the side of a barn (see photo top left). In the house, the shed became a large, modern living space. In the garage, it became a play space for my teenage children.

I decided to make a clear distinction between the rear, more private side of the house (see photo p. 96) and the front, more public side. The rear is modern, with large expanses of glass facing the woods. The front is traditional-looking, with smaller windows and an open porch (see photo bottom left). The house was sited to align with the street, similar to its neighbors, but set back slightly to afford total privacy in the rear. Looking out from the inside, you see only trees and wildlife; the neighbors' houses are out of view.

Careful Planning Gets the Most out of 2,400 sq. ft.

Careful planning was key to achieving the sense of openness and modernism I was after. The house has a simple 24-ft. by 26-ft., three-story gabled core with a 24-ft. by 36-ft. loftlike living space (see floor plans p. 102). The bedrooms, playroom loft, bath-

The living, dining, and music areas (see photo above) are more loosely organized within the large, open living area. The extensive glass makes these spaces appear to flow directly to cedar decks on the front and back, creating a strong relationship between the inside and outside. With their edges defined by pine trees, wild blueberry bushes, and beech trees, outdoor garden spaces become natural extensions of interior living spaces.

Clear-pine brackets and columns, fir ceilings, ponderosa-pine windows and doors, and white-ash stairs and floors all were carefully chosen for their intended use (see also photo p. 103). Photo taken at D on floor plan.

rooms, kitchen, laundry, and closets are tightly organized on the three levels of the core house. I used space-saving details throughout, such as tall bookshelves doubling as walls, to conceal both stairways (see photo p. 100). I also placed a wide built-in desk along the edge of the loft instead of a wall or handrail, which makes the room appear more open. The bathrooms and laundry are grouped together on the front of the house with small windows for privacy. The bedrooms are in the back, with large windows looking out to the woods.

Does a Lot of Glass Mean High Utility Bills?

The large glass panels on the rear add to the feeling of spaciousness, but I'm often asked about heating bills. Several strategies helped to offset heat loss through the glass. First, the two-story core house is energy-efficient and inexpensive to heat. During the design process, I eliminated about 10 windows that were planned for the core house. I removed them partly to save money but also because

I thought the large amount of glass on the rear of the house would more than compensate for forgoing windows in every wall of every room. The insulated-glass windows are argon-filled with a low-E coating, which is energy-efficient and readily available.

Second, the house is heated with an oil-fired, radiant-floor heating system, which is also efficient and cost effective. Due to ledge rock close to the surface of much of the building site, I decided on a concrete

This space created by a room without walls enables the dining **(1)** (see photo left, taken at E on floor plan) and kitchen **(2)** (see photo above, taken at F on floor plan) areas each to benefit from the common space that's created. Sunlight reflects off colorful ash-veneer cabinets and the stainless-steel refrigerator panel, animating and warming the space.

slab-on-grade floor instead of blasting for a basement. The radiant heating is set in the concrete slab, which is insulated from below. This slab acts as a heat sink, releasing heat over time and offsetting variations in temperature.

Third, the amount of glass, the windows' southern orientation, and the roof overhangs all were designed and calculated to provide passive-solar heating. In the summer, the roof overhangs shade the large windows from the sun. During the winter, when the angle of the sun is lower, the roof design allows the sun's heat to penetrate deeply into the house. Once inside the house, the heat is absorbed by the floor and radiates back into the living space. Consequently, the heating bills for my house are lower than those of most similarly sized houses.

Natural wood helps to create a sense of warmth and comfort in a home.

LIVING ARRANGEMENT IS SYNCHRONIZED WITH THE SUN

To gain solar advantage, the second-floor bedrooms and the open living/dining area all face south with large glass windows and doors. The bedrooms are positioned on the eastern end of the house, and a large triangular window funnels evening sun into the living/dining area. The bathrooms and laundry room are on the well-insulated north side, where there are few windows.

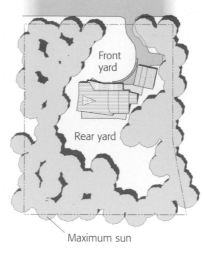

Front yard

Rear yard

Maximum sun

Stair to loft

Second floor

Dn

Kids' playroom

Open to below

A

Bedroom   Bedroom

Third-floor loft

Garage

Laundry

Entry   ← G

D

Deck

Up

F

Mechanicals

Mudroom/closet

Living/dining area   ← C

E

Kitchen

Master bedroom

Closet

B

Deck

First floor

North

0   4   8   16 ft.

Photos taken at lettered positions.

SPECS

BEDROOMS: 3

BATHROOMS: 2

SIZE: 2,400 sq. ft.

COST: $100.00 per sq. ft.

COMPLETED: 1998

LOCATION: Yarmouth, Maine

ARCHITECT: Scott Simons

DESIGNER: Mark Dorsey Inc.

Wooden Finishes Add Warmth to a Large Open Space

Natural wood helps to create a sense of warmth and comfort in a home. A variety of wood species was used in this house for this purpose. The exterior is finished with white-cedar shingles, red-cedar trim, and white-cedar decking. On the interior, clear-pine brackets and turned columns support the exposed main carrying beams, which are off-the-shelf 2x12 Microllam beams.

The high ceiling in the main living area is covered with clear-finished fir paneling, and the doors and windows are ponderosa pine. They're trimmed with simple clear-pine casings and moldings. The floors and stairs are clear-finished white ash (see photo facing page).

Each species of wood was considered carefully for its intended use, and colors and finishes were coordinated to complement the whole. The kitchen cabinets and dining-room shelving are white-ash veneer plywood with clear-, green-, and gray-stained finishes (see photo right p. 101). The interior and exterior doors are oak veneer with clear- and green-stained finishes. I had a lot of fun choosing colors and finishes for the woodwork, often including my teenagers in the process. We were looking for variety and playfulness. Green is my favorite color, so it naturally found its way into the house in several places.

Common Materials Used Creatively

The house is composed of common, economical materials combined in simple yet creative ways. Although most of the framing is typical of a wood-frame house with 2x6 exterior walls, I carefully considered the dimensions in the core house to keep

Natural-wood finishes make a space more intimate. Photo taken at C on floor plan.

framing-lumber sizes smaller and more economical, such as 2x10 joists versus 2x12s.

I held down costs on exterior and interior trim pieces by using stock sizes and simple profiles. I placed few windows on the front of the house, partly to save money but also to create contrast with the rear of the house. The garage is also simple; it's no more than a shingled box with a sliding barn door.

For the roof, I used Galvalume, an inexpensive coated sheet steel. It was the closest material I could find to an old tin barn roof that had a decent warranty. It cost about $2.50 more per sq. ft. than an asphalt-shingle roof but was well worth it. It captures the feeling of traditional northern New England barns, and it sheds snow beautifully.

From the street, the modern quality and lines of the house are subtle. Its shape, detailing, and appearance comfortably fit this traditional New England village, yet the house embodies the finest qualities of spacious, modern living. The house has per-

formed beautifully through several severe winters. It is a transforming experience each day to walk through the front door and look across the open, modern living space to the woods behind the house.

Since the completion of this house, my firm and I have designed others in northern New England using many of the same planning and design principles. Some of our clients have been initially reluctant to build soaring, open spaces, fearing that they would sacrifice intimacy. In this house, though, they see that open living spaces can be cozy. Traditional house design doesn't have to mean small boxes under a peaked roof.

Scott Simons lives in Yarmouth, Maine, with his two children, Althea and Will. He has a ten person architectural practice in Portland, Maine.

Red House

I F YOU WANT TO WORK IN JACKSON HOLE, WYOMING, YOU might end up living in Idaho. That's because houses are a lot more affordable just over the pass in Victor, 24 miles away. But that can be a harrowing 24 miles, especially on a winter night. My wife, Peggy, and I made the drive one day to go house-hunting, and on the way back to our rental house in Jackson, she said she'd rather move back to New York City than make that drive every day.

So we concentrated on finding the nearly impossible: an affordable building site in Wilson, a little town a few miles west of Jackson Hole. Wilson is a quirky mix of old-time ranchers, former hippies turned businesspeople, and every variety of mountain junkies from well-heeled trust-funders to dishwashers with three jobs and six roommates. It's the kind of place I've always wanted to call home.

Our dream of a sloping site on a wooded hill with streams and wildflowers turned out to be just that: a dream. After a quick reality check, we set our sights on the valley floor, where a new subdivision was being carved out of an old hayfield. There were lots more buyers than lots, so we put our name in the lottery hat and were lucky enough to draw a good number. To be honest, we would have been happy with any patch of dirt that the bank would underwrite, but we ended up with a great corner lot that others had passed over because it was on a corner. Some saw it as a drawback because of the extra exposure to the street. We saw it as an asset that would let us put the house up front and set the garage to the side (see photo inset above).

A B O V E The corner-lot advantage. Both house and garage are close to the street, which is a real advantage in a snowy climate. Photo taken at A on floor plan. **R I G H T** Sheds, gables, an angled chimney and a compound slope on the porch roof energize the western elevation. Photo taken at B on floor plan.

A New Angle on an Old House

We started with a tight budget and a rough image: a simple farmhouse like the ones that used to be common in this valley. We wanted the house to have a metal roof, a deep porch to escape the summer sun, and a crackling fireplace to combat the winter chill. This image led us to a two-story gabled structure with bedrooms and bathrooms upstairs and the kitchen, sunroom, laundry, and pantry below (see floor plans facing page). A shed-roofed living/dining room abuts the rear of the house.

Our public living/dining room is wide open to the outdoors and to the neighborhood. We can drink in the last rays of the setting sun through the large west-facing windows, and our friends can wave to us while we sit at the table as they cross-country ski along the adjacent bike path.

TAPERED DECK AND CONCRETE AT THE CORE

Along the west side of the house, a tapering deck leads to the mudroom, which occupies the western half of a concrete-block corridor that slices through the house. Upstairs, the central hall leads to the bedrooms. Note how two doors lead to one room for the kids. One day, it will become two, separated by a closet wall. In the hall, a rail-mounted ladder provides access to loft spaces over the bedrooms.

Loft

Ladder — Storage

Loft play space

Hall

Loft office

Ladder to the loft spaces rides this rail.

SPECS

BEDROOMS: **3**

BATHROOMS: **2½**

SIZE: **1,900 sq. ft., including lofts**

COST: **$95.00 per sq. ft.**

COMPLETED: **1999**

LOCATION: **Wilson, Wyoming**

ARCHITECTS: **Paul and Peggy Duncker**

BUILDERS: **Paul and Peggy Duncker**

Second floor

Future closet partition

Bedroom

Hall

Bedroom

Dn

Master bedroom

North

0 2 4 8 ft.

Photos taken at lettered positions.

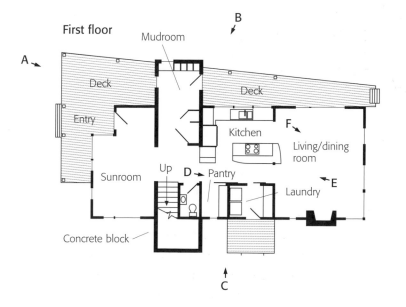

First floor

Mudroom

B

A

Deck

Deck

Entry

Kitchen

F

Sunroom

Up

D

Pantry

Living/dining room

E

Laundry

Concrete block

C

ABOVE Cohesive color and texture. On the east side, the landing to the second floor sits atop a split-faced concrete-block cube. The gray board-and-batten siding above the blocks and the steely corrugated roofing (see sources) create a subtle palette of related colors and textures. Photo taken at C on floor plan.

A generous porch wraps around the two most public faces of the house. The porch tapers along the west side of the house, resulting in a distinctively angled roofline (see photo p. 105). Midway, the porch roof covers a bump-out that penetrates the house's wall near the kitchen. Made of insulated concrete block, this bump-out contains the mudroom and is part of a long, narrow concrete-block enclosure that emerges on both sides of the building (see photo p. 106). Using the exposed concrete blocks, which support the stair landing on the east side of the house, helps to tie the house to the tradition of local agricultural buildings.

A House Built Like a Beer Cooler

The roof and walls of our house are made of structural insulated panels (SIPs), which are close cousins to the stuff that keeps drinks cold in a picnic cooler and warm in a foam coffee cup. The panels (see Sources p. 111) that we used are 10½ in. thick on the roof, for an R-40 rating, and the walls are 6½ in. thick (R-26). Each panel is made up of an expanded-polystyrene core sandwiched between layers of ½-in. thick structural skins of oriented strand board (see photo below).

In addition to the high insulating value of SIPs, the fact that every exterior wall has structural sheathing on both sides is in our favor. Heavy snow loads and an active earthquake zone have combined to make for some tough code requirements around here. The SIPs easily meet or exceed them. Furthermore, once the panels come off the truck, they can be assembled in a fraction of the time required to stick-frame a comparable building. Our house went from subfloor to completed roof in nine days with a crew of four. Cedar clapboards (barn red, of course) give the newfangled walls an old-fashioned look.

ABOVE SIPs made of OSB go up ASAP. Structural insulated panels (expanded-polystyrene foam insulation sandwiched between two layers of oriented strand board) make for a tight, highly insulated house shell. As they are assembled, the panels are glued together into a single unit.

ABOVE Concrete block and a crackling fire. Although it is wrapped in rural imagery
on the outside, the interior of the house is definitely modern. Crisp white walls played against
split-faced concrete block surround the fireplace. Big windows with transoms overlook
the Grand Tetons to the north. Photo taken at F on floor plan.

Steel Trim, Aluminum Grout

I've been a cabinetmaker longer than I've been an architect, so I appreciate the way things are assembled. I saw our house as a way to work a variety of materials into the mix. In our kitchen, for example, the curved countertop is clear-coated plate steel (see photos above and right taken at D and E on floor plan). The kitchen cabinets and the interior doors are made of red birch with wired glass.

Upstairs, I slipped some aluminum into the floor. There, we used ¾-in. birch plywood cut into big tiles as the finished flooring (photo 1). The seams between the tiles are filled with thin bar stock. In the tiny half-bath under the stairs, wired-glass risers act as a segmented skylight to illuminate the room (photo 2). In other places, steel angle stock turns into a trim element that separates concrete block from drywall (photo 3). —P. D.

1

2

3

Living with a Heat Pump

The one drawback we've found to our ground-source geothermal heat-pump system is the noise. Our heat pump is below the stairwell in the center of our house and stands directly on the subfloor. When the unit kicks on, the sounds and vibrations of the compressor (in the noise range of a large commercial restaurant freezer) are transmitted throughout the whole house via the subfloor.

You can avoid this problem by installing a heat pump on a separate slab in the crawlspace or in an attached garage. The plumbing system also should be vibration-isolated by using short sections of flexible hose at the unit connections. You'll sleep better, all night. —P. D.

I saw our house as a way to work a variety of materials into the mix.

Concrete Floors Warmed by the Earth

Inside the house, rural imagery gives way to contemporary detailing (see photos facing page). We wanted honest materials, exposed hardware and connections, and durable finishes—important when half of the occupants of the house are 8-year-old Alexandra and 11-year-old Christopher. Soccer balls, skateboards, books, Legos, and cat toys seem to make up roughly half of the mass of our house. With this in mind, we chose an indestructible concrete-slab floor for the downstairs. It is finished with two coats of boiled linseed oil and is heated by way of hot water running through polyethylene tubing embedded in the slab.

To heat the water, we chose a ground-source geothermal heat pump. This technology allows us to extract heat from the ground using only the amount of electricity needed by the pumps and compressor. Warm floors are a wonderful way to heat a house, and we would choose this solution again in a heartbeat. We would, however, make an important change in the location of the geothermal heat pump (see sidebar above).

Some Bedrooms Are Still Evolving

The upstairs bedrooms are small but comfortable, with a master suite on the north side and one large room for the kids on the south. The kids' room currently has two doors into it, and the room has no closet. The plan is to build a long wall of cabinetry to divide the room into two and to incorporate built-in closets and desks.

Until the day that the Britney Spears half of the room has to be acoustically separated from the Jimi Hendrix half, the kids like each other's company.

And just in case you're wondering: Yes, the house is named after our favorite Jimi Hendrix song.

Paul and Peggy Duncker are architects in Jackson Hole, Wyoming. Rather than work together, they've decided to stay married. Paul has a design/build firm called HandsOn; Peggy is a partner in Tobler Duncker Architects.

SOURCES

Una-Clad
(corrugated-steel roofing)
(800) 426-7737
www.unaclad.com

Insulspan
(structural insulated panels)
P.O. Box 38
9012 East U.S. 223
Blissfield, MI 49228
(800) 726-3510
www.insulspan.com

Wirsbo
(polyethylene Pex tubing)
(800) 321-4739
www.wirsbo.com

Designing a Historical House

FOR ONE AUGUST DAY IN 1814, TINY BROOKEVILLE, MARYLAND, was the capital of the nation. Here, President James Madison escaped the British invasion of Washington, D.C., during the War of 1812. When Rich and Pam Chandler asked me to design a house for their lot in Brookeville, I knew that brush with history would complicate the project. My design had to win the Chandlers' approval, and the county Historic Preservation Commission had to approve it as well.

What the Owners Want

Rich and Pam's interior program was simple: They wanted a large, rustic family room with a fireplace (see photo p. 114) a formal dining room and an eat-in kitchen that could double as a conversation area when they entertained (see photo top p. 115). They asked for a small study on the first floor, an office and three bedrooms. Rounding out the owners' wish list were a covered porch (see photo bottom p. 115) and a garden close to the kitchen (see photo p. 117).

Rich and Pam were adamant that the project include a two-car garage and a place to turn around vehicles (see photo top p. 119). Their street dead-ends at the house, and without a way to turn around cars, they would have to back 500 ft. down a narrow gravel road.

Planned to look like an older house added to over time. Varied window sizes, a gable with a parapet and a single stone chimney earmark a series of so-called additions. Photo taken at A on floor plan.

Salvaged ceiling timbers add an aura of age. In the fictional history of the house, this oldest wing retains the original framing and fireplace. Photo taken at E on floor plan.

The Chandlers had strong feelings about the exterior finish. At our first meeting, they showed me photographs of several buildings with stuccoed exteriors. Rich liked the uneven appearance of stucco as it weathers.

Working with the builder, Doug Horsman of Horsman Homes Inc., I started to develop a design that I hoped would suit the owners and satisfy the concerns of the commission. In my early sketches, I ended up with a two-story, 3,000-sq.-ft. home with a two-car detached garage.

What the Historic Preservation Commission Wants

The commission had its own list of requirements. The first was that all buildings be positioned at the 40-ft. front-yard setback line to align with an adjacent home.

To create the rustic living room, we used an exposed plank-and-beam ceiling supported by salvaged hand-hewn timbers.

ABOVE **Eat-in kitchen.** When the homeowners are entertaining, guests can sit and visit the chef. Photo taken at D on floor plan.

Because a conservation easement split the lot, only the front half of the lot could be built on. The ¾-acre lot was starting to seem small.

Even more restrictive was the commission's size limitation for any house on the site. The building's footprint couldn't exceed 1,200 sq. ft., and the overall size could be no more than 2,400 sq. ft. The commission wouldn't approve more than a single-car garage, detached from the house and preferably set back from the street. We were encouraged to borrow more from the federal style. The idea of a stucco facade among the brick Federal-style buildings of Brookeville seemed unacceptable to the commission. Finding middle ground wasn't going to be easy.

ABOVE **East-facing porch is a shady spot on a hot afternoon.** Overlooking a conservation easement, the porch is also a great spot for watching wildlife at dawn. Photo taken at C on floor plan.

Designing an Old House

After several iterations and seemingly endless consultations, the commission approved a design with 2,300 sq. ft. of living space on two floors (see photo p. 118). Three bedrooms, two baths and the laundry were on the second floor, and other living spaces were on ground level. A two-story open hall included the stair (see photo below) and a door to a courtyard and the garage. We kept the stucco but, to please the commission, changed the arched masonry over the windows that was in earlier plans to flat lintels that reflected Federal-style stone lintels.

I designed the Chandler house to create the impression that the entire building was not built at the same time but had been altered over the years. I think this look of a house grown with time is a big part of why the commission approved the design.

Stairs abut the stone wall of the old house. The transom above the passage to the family room suggests the location of an original front door. Photo taken at G on floor plan.

I invented a history of the house. Originally, it had been a stone two-story structure set parallel to the street. A large fireplace dominated one end. This original house is visible today in the exposed, hewn framing and the stone fireplace in the family room.

The first addition to the old stone dwelling houses the kitchen, the stairwell, an upstairs laundry, and a bath. Part of the stone exterior wall of the original house is visible from the stairwell, but generally, the finish here is more refined than in the older section. A transom above the passage between the family room and the entry hall suggests the location of the former front door. The final addition contains the dining room, study, and two bedrooms, and is at the front of the house. Its north wall jogs in a few feet, differentiating it from the previous addition. Also, this jog helps the house to meet the size requirement imposed by the commission. The cut was made in the study and the bedroom above because the Chandlers thought these rooms could best afford to lose the space.

Friends Come to the Side Door

At this point, neither the Chandlers nor I wanted a front door because it would open into the dining room or the downsized study. But this arrangement concerned the commission, which wanted a front door facing the street. The Chandlers were content with the two entry doors leading to the courtyard but agreed to this third door to please the commission. Opening into the study, this door reduces the useful size of the room.

An unexpected benefit, however, came of the front door. Because the door doesn't lead into a traffic area, friends and family know to use the side doors. A knock on the front door announces a stranger's presence.

A cutting garden outside the kitchen. The walls show the effect of an acid wash, which gave the stucco a weathered look. Photo taken at F on floor plan.

To the south lies a fenced garden (see photo above). The Chandlers are both gardeners, and this spot is convenient to the kitchen. I imagine it to be the remnant of a larger kitchen garden belonging to the original house.

Windows That Aren't

Our proposal included a stucco-finished facade that would look like parging over old stonework. The shapes of stone lintels and sills (actually cast stone), an element common to the Federal-style houses so admired by the commission, remain exposed.

The house is conventionally framed, with a veneer of 4-in. concrete blocks. The stucco was troweled over the concrete-block veneer. Doug worked closely with the plasterer tinting the stucco mix. After the final coat set, muriatic acid diluted 5 parts water to 1 part acid was sprayed on with a hand-pumped insecticide sprayer to age the stucco. After spraying the entire house, Doug rinsed off the acid with a garden hose.

The terne metal roof is field-painted and hand-seamed. Its slightly uneven coloring complements the textured stucco. Similar roofs are common in Brookeville, which adds another historic connection.

DESIGNED TO RESEMBLE A HOUSE THAT WAS ADDED TO OVER TIME

In the author's fictional history of the project, the original farmhouse, with a massive stone chimney, lies to the rear. It is abutted by two subsequent additions, the first containing the kitchen and stairs. The second consists of the dining room and study.

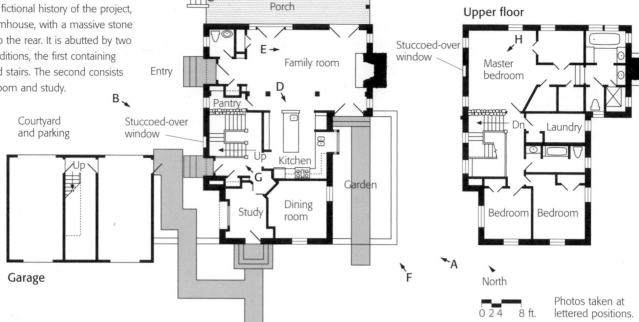

Main floor — Porch, Family room, Entry, Pantry, Kitchen, Study, Dining room, Garden, Up, Courtyard and parking, Garage, Stuccoed-over window

Upper floor — Master bedroom, Laundry, Bedroom, Bedroom, Stuccoed-over window, Dn

North

Photos taken at lettered positions.
0 2 4 8 ft.

On the master bedroom's north wall and in the stairwell, stuccoed-over windows are visible from outside (see top photo facing page). They appear to be part of an older window pattern. But, the fiction goes, as happens in older houses, the rooms changed to a more private function, and the windows were closed off. This device allowed me to space the windows rhythmically and left enough interior wall space to place a bed in the master bedroom (see bottom photo facing page).

Doug and I furthered the impression of a house that had been added to over its life with secondhand materials. For example, to create the rustic living room, we used an exposed plank-and-beam ceiling supported by salvaged hand-hewn timbers. Doug spent hours culling through salvage yards to locate these beams. Recycled heart-pine flooring was laid throughout the first floor.

The Chandlers opted for old exterior doors, touring salvage companies for just the right ones. They found doors from buildings in Philadelphia and in England.

A Carriage House Is History's Garage

I finally got the commission to accept a two-car detached garage by designing it to mimic an earlier carriage house. The garage is set tight to the front-yard setback, slightly forward of the house. This placement satisfied the commission's desire to have the front of the house align with the neighboring home. The garage is only 11 ft. away from the house's sidewall. Opposing doors on the garage and the house make travel between the buildings a matter of a few quick steps.

The driveway leads beyond the garage to a courtyard separating it from the house. The courtyard is large enough to turn vehicles around in and allowed me to put the garage doors to the back. I'm sure the location of the doors helped to win the commission's approval because garage doors are in no way a Federal element.

To further the illusion of a carriage house, I added false barn doors to the front of the garage. An open-air passageway through the center of the garage suggests a stable.

ABOVE Courtyard provides a turnaround for cars. Garage doors face away from the street to maintain a facade acceptable to the local historic preservation committee. Photo taken at B on floor plan.

LEFT Master bedroom views the original stone wall. A fictional window whose shape is still visible from the back of the house was covered over to make space for the bed. Photo taken at H on floor plan.

I designed the Chandler house to create the impression that the entire building was not built at the same time but had been altered over the years.

A secondary feature of the garage borrows from the loft spaces often found above carriage houses. Space for a guest bedroom and an office had been lost when the house was downsized. Both of these rooms can be added later in spaces that might have once contained hay and tack.

The detached garage led me to a design element I think adds to the house's facade. With the carriage house positioned away from the main house, there is an open area between the buildings. This area, and the open passage through the carriage house, are what I call view slots. They give glimpses of the courtyard beyond from the street.

Almost a year to the day after I started work on the Chandler house, the commission approved the design. Their vote wasn't unanimous, but a majority agreed that the project was respectful of the historic community. The clients seem happy, too.

Kevin McKenna is an architect from Columbia, Maryland. He owns a studio specializing in residential design for new homes and renovations. His firm can be reached at www.Kevinmckenna-architect.com

A California Home Designed with the Future in Mind

WHEN MY ELDERLY FATHER ASKED ME TO DESIGN HIS new house, he was adamant about one thing: The house had to be red. My father needed a small house with a second-floor bedroom that would encourage him to use the stairs for exercise for as long as possible, and a first-floor bedroom for the day when the stairs proved to be too much. And the house had to be red.

We found a small, vacant lot in downtown Berkeley, California. A flat rectangle with none of the views cherished in the hilly East Bay area, the lot was conveniently close to the senior-citizens center. A looming three-story apartment building next door helped to define the house's L-shape footprint. The long side of the house blocks off as much of the apartment building as possible, and the short side of the house creates a garden courtyard that was oriented to the warm, inviting southwest.

My father liked a house I had designed several years earlier that had intersecting groin-vaulted roofs. However, such unusual framing was beyond the budget for this house, so we used simpler, barrel-vaulted roofs over the living room and master bedrooms (see sidebar p. 125).

Shape of the house forms a courtyard. The L-shape floor plan of the house was designed to block the views of a neighboring apartment building and to enclose a garden that takes advantage of the lot's southern exposure. Photo taken at A on floor plan.

Kitchen illuminated from above. Skylights above the staircase and kitchen create a sundial effect as the day progresses. A curved soffit over the stove adds a sculptural element that echoes the ceilings. Photo taken at B on floor plan.

Sunlight Determines the Floor Plan

In most conventional architecture, daylighting is an accidental byproduct of style. Windows are placed where they are stylistically expected as viewed from the exterior. The opposite approach applies to this house, where the play of natural light is an essential design factor that largely dictates both the floor and site plans as well as the placement of the windows.

Early-morning light for some people is as necessary as coffee, but my father is not an early riser. So the three-story building that blocked the first rays of the sun was not a real problem for him. By midmorning, the first light illuminates the master bathroom on the second floor through a 3½-ft. by 6-ft. skylight over the shower, and there isn't a nicer way to start the day. The main windows in both bedrooms and the living room (see photo right) face south so that sunlight penetrates a few feet into the rooms in the summer and reaches all the way across the house in the winter. Two tall slit windows on the west wall of the living room catch the last rays of the sun in the evenings. Sunlight cascading down from the skylight that is located at the top of the stairwell (see photo facing page) serves as an informal sundial.

Tinted Plasters Make the House Glow

Once the house was closed in, we started to work with the exterior stucco. None of the commercially available mixes came anywhere close to the right shade of red. We made test batches and ended up with various shades of pastel pink. All were wrong.

So we decided to use a technique known as al fresco, one perfected during the Renaissance. After conventional scratch and brown coats are applied, a finish coat of

Plaster finishes and vaulted ceilings create a simple elegance. The main living area's high, curved ceilings and tall windows allow natural light to play on the mottled plaster walls, even during a foggy morning. Photo taken at C on floor plan.

The play of natural light is an essential design factor that largely dictates both the floor and site plans as well as the placement of the windows.

plaster is troweled on, smoothed, and, while it is still wet, painted with lime-fast pigments that have been mixed in water. The pigments chemically bind with the carbonating lime crystals as the plaster cures. The result is a fresco, a permanent watercolor. Instead of the finish coat of lime-and-marble-dust mixture used in the 15th century, we substituted a modern mix of lime, sand, and white cement. This mixture reduces the available time for coloring but makes for a harder finished surface.

On the interior, we used a setting-type gypsum-based plaster (not to be confused with ready-mix joint compound) applied over blue board. Gypsum-based plaster resists forces up to 3,000 psi, which made it possible to eliminate metallic corner beads that seem out of place on a rustic plaster job. We mixed equal amounts of sand and

gypsum plaster and applied several layers to the walls, which resulted in a textured, mottled finish that varied in color from pure white to a light, soft gray. This mix became the base color for the interior. The fireplace and stairwell walls were later color-washed with pigments and water and then sealed with an acrylic sealer.

We treated other walls with a basic whitewash: 1 part lime putty (hydrated lime and water) that was further diluted with 2 to 3 parts water. As seen on the living-room walls (see photo p. 123) whitewash refracts light in a way that no paint can match. It is a fairly fragile finish that's not for everyone, however. Due to its porous, water-soluble surface, it can't be washed; the lime wash must be reapplied periodically. Fortunately, the process is very easy, one that makes painting look difficult.

FINDING PRIVACY IN A DENSE NEIGHBORHOOD

Sited on a tight urban lot with no views, the L-shape plan of the house turns its back on a three-story apartment building to the east. The majority of the house's windows face south and look into the courtyard formed by the right-angle footprint. Inside, the living area is a large high-ceilinged space divided by a kneewall and counter peninsula. The two bedroom suites, one on each floor, are in the southern wing.

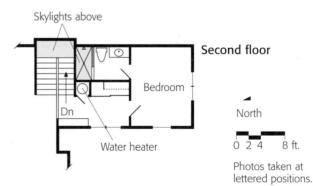

Second floor

North

0 2 4 8 ft.

Photos taken at lettered positions.

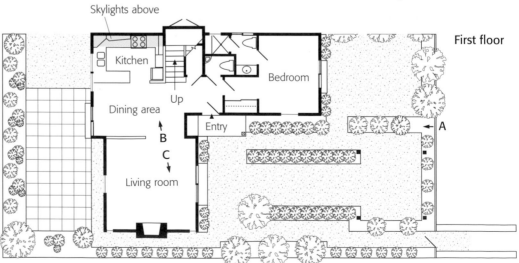

First floor

SPECS

BEDROOMS: 2

BATHROOMS: 2½

SIZE: 1,231 sq. ft.

COST: $100.00 per sq. ft.

COMPLETED: 1997

LOCATION: Berkeley, California

ARCHITECTS:

Bruce and Colette Kelley

BUILDER: Gleason and Tankard

Making a Curved Roof the Easy Way

The framing for a cylindrical vault is straightforward: The rafters are supported by curving top plates cut from straight stock. This method produces a fairer curve than laminating plates, whose curves tend to flatten out at the ends.

After laying out the radius on 2x8s, the framers cut and nailed the curving sections together, making a curved top plate. Once the gable ends were framed, 2x12 rafters were dropped into joist hangers nailed at right angles to the radius. Blocking was installed wherever the rafter length exceeded 10 ft.; the bays were insulated with R-30 fiberglass batts. —B. K.

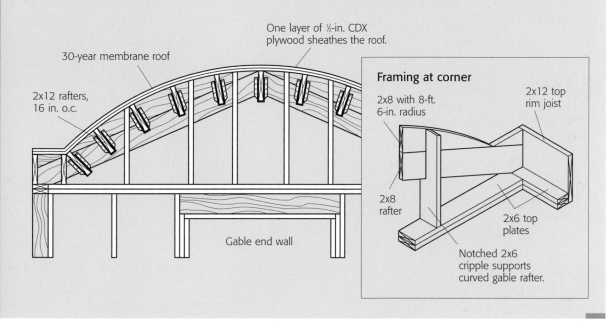

30-year membrane roof

One layer of ½-in. CDX plywood sheathes the roof.

2x12 rafters, 16 in. o.c.

Gable end wall

Framing at corner

2x8 with 8-ft. 6-in. radius

2x12 top rim joist

2x8 rafter

2x6 top plates

Notched 2x6 cripple supports curved gable rafter.

Making the House Fit an Elderly Client

For those designing a house for an elderly person, consider making some simple design adjustments and structural refinements to make his or her life a little easier. For instance, by building on a low slab one step above grade, we were able to create an easy entry that could be modified for wheelchair access on short notice. In the bathrooms, we used grab bars instead of towel bars and installed extensive blocking where other grab bars might be needed. The floor plan included a bedroom suite on each floor, intended for the day when the stairs

became too risky. The stairs themselves were built with a 7-in. riser and an 11-in. tread. These dimensions make a stairway that is safer for the elderly and that feels considerably more gracious.

Bruce Kelley and his wife, Colette, have designed U.S. and world champion sailboats, power yachts, furniture, landscapes, and award winning homes. Their architectural practice is in Berkeley, California.

Texas
Saddlebag House

ABOUT AN HOUR'S DRIVE SOUTH OF THE DALLAS–FORT WORTH sprawl lies the sultry Texas flatland where most houses have grazing cattle instead of lawn ornaments. In the heart of this region, near the town of Eureka, two rivers were dammed to form the Richland-Chambers Reservoir.

Besides quenching the thirst of those big cities to the north, this lake and others like it have begun to attract vacation-minded Texans looking for relief from the angry summer heat. It was the promise of cool breezes off the lake that prompted the Spragues to contact me about designing a lakeside vacation house for them.

A One-Story House That Looks Taller

Because Charles and Alayne Sprague were both retired, they wanted a home on one level so they wouldn't have to deal with stairs. But all the nearby houses were at least two stories tall. So my first task was to design a one-story house that wouldn't look out of place among its taller neighbors.

I started with a fairly simple rectangular plan (see floor plans p. 133). To give the house a taller appearance, I put the roof over this section at a 60-degree pitch (approximately 21-in-12). This steep pitch placed the peak at about the same level as the peak of a two-story house with a shallower-pitched roof.

To break up this steep plane, I placed several shed roofs at a much shallower 30-degree pitch (approximately 7-in-12). But instead of creating typical shed dormers, I let the sheds spill like saddlebags out beyond the sides of the main house (see photo facing page). More shed dormers ride piggyback style atop the saddlebag dormers. In some cases, the piggyback dormers run all the way to the outside walls. In others, they stop short of the outside walls to form smaller dormers.

Tall in the saddle. Built in a neighborhood of two-story houses, this one-story house uses a steeply pitched central roof and a brick-veneered gable to make the house look taller. Photo taken at B on floor plan.

ABOVE Texas-size screened porch. This enclosed porch can seat a large family at a Texas barbecue with plenty of room left for the kids to play. Large sliding doors make the porch accessible from the living room and the master bedroom. Photo taken at C on floor plan.

Interesting Ceiling Planes Inside

The biggest of the shed roofs covers a roomy screened porch (see photo above). At the top of Alayne Sprague's wish list, the porch had to be big enough to accommodate dinner for their large, extended family while having enough room for the kids to play board games. Fitting it in under one of

the saddlebags gave the porch lots of room without having it look like an appendage to the house. While breaking up the lines of the house on the outside, the sheds' interiors allow for plenty of clerestory windows that let light into the rooms. Dramatic planes are created as the ceilings in the saddlebags meet the steeper central ceiling (see photo facing page).

Soaring shapes in drywall. Exciting ceiling planes are created as the shallower shed roofs intersect with the much steeper central roof. To the left above, the kids' loft overlooks the grown ups' area. Photo taken at I on floor plan.

Ventilation without the bugs. Glass doors open onto a screened porch to capture breezes and views of the lake. Photo taken at A on floor plan.

I placed the bedrooms at the ends of the house on both sides of a spacious great room. The living-room side of the great room has large sliding-glass doors that open onto the porch for cross ventilation and for views of the lake (see photo left). The master bedroom at the east end of the house also has sliding doors that open onto the porch (see photo top facing page). The master bath is tucked in neatly under one of the saddlebags.

The two guest bedrooms at the west end of the house wrap around a shared bathroom. These rooms are the only ones in the house that have flat ceilings, although the ceiling in each bedroom is broken up with a clerestory (see bottom left photo facing page). These clerestories extend into two sleeping lofts for the grandkids; the lofts are accessible only by ladder. Each of the lofts has a viewing port overlooking the great room and the adult world below (see bottom right photo facing page).

Glulams Hold Things Together

The open interior of the house created some unique building challenges. To maintain structural integrity, I placed large glulam beams strategically throughout the house. We saved the expense of sanding and finishing beams and collar ties by covering them with drywall wherever they were exposed.

We were fortunate to have Philip Crowell, a local contractor, working on the house. Philip's extensive lakefront building experience gave him a leg up on dealing with soil conditions and the high water table that typically plague many lakeside building sites. The house was built on a 5-in. structural slab poured over 25 concrete piers buried 20 ft. deep into the Texas clay. The slab was eventually saw-cut into a grid pattern and stained to form the finished floor.

LEFT **The master bedroom uses tall ceilings** to make the room feel more spacious. Photo taken at F on floor plan.

BOTTOM LEFT **The bedrooms are at opposite ends.** The guest bedroom is tucked under one of the shed outcroppings. Photo taken at E on floor plan.

BOTTOM RIGHT **Loft with a view, kids only.** A kids' sleeping loft upstairs is accessible by ladder. Viewing ports look over the adults' great room. Photo taken at G on floor plan.

ABOVE **Stacked-up sheds.** To break up the steep roof plane and to expand the floor plan, the architect added spaces under shed roofs. Photo taken at H on floor plan.

ABOVE **Far-out building.** Using a variant of the roof that shelters the house, the architect created this two-car garage as a separate building. Photo taken at D on floor plan.

A Separate Garage Mimics the House

The 1-acre lot that the Spragues chose was dotted with 100-year-old oak trees, making it an oasis compared with most of the neighboring lots. We were able to site the house so that it would be nestled among the trees, giving the house a measure of shade from the intense summer heat (see photo above).

Deed restrictions required that the house be covered with a certain percentage of masonry. So we put brick veneer over the end walls of the house, which helps to

BUILDING ON A BASIC RECTANGLE

Starting with a rectangular shape, the architect packed extra spaces he calls saddlebags onto the sides to expand the rooms and to keep the plan (except the shaded area that indicates a children's sleeping loft) on one level.

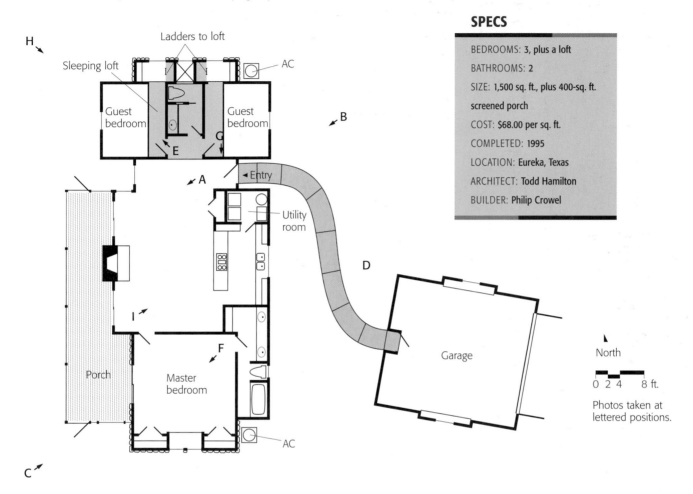

SPECS

BEDROOMS: 3, plus a loft

BATHROOMS: 2

SIZE: 1,500 sq. ft., plus 400-sq. ft. screened porch

COST: $68.00 per sq. ft.

COMPLETED: 1995

LOCATION: Eureka, Texas

ARCHITECT: Todd Hamilton

BUILDER: Philip Crowel

Photos taken at lettered positions.

emphasize the height of the house. The saddlebags were covered with vertical board-and-batten siding painted white. Green roof shingles give the house a colorful accent.

Another of the Spragues' requests was to have a separate two-car garage tied to the house with a serpentine walk (see bottom photo facing page). This separation gave Alayne a place for wildflower gardens. The oak-tree canopy above turns this space into a lovely outdoor room.

As a playful gesture, I had the exterior of the garage mimic the house, but I did it in reverse. Instead of having smaller saddlebags spilling off the main gable structure,

the garage has two full-length saddlebags that cradle the middle section. To intensify that effect, I stopped the central gable on the garage a couple of feet above the ground with the board-and-batten siding running below. The result gives the garage a hot-dog-in-a-bun look.

Todd Hamilton practices in Dallas, Texas, and teaches architecture at the University of Texas at Arlington.

Instead of creating typical shed dormers, I let the sheds spill like saddlebags out beyond the sides of the main house.

Built Intending to Stay

TWELVE YEARS AGO, A DESIGNER FRIEND MADE ME A business proposition. He had invested a great deal of effort for a client, seeking the city's approval to build houses on three lots at the edge of an old subdivision. Objections from neighbors long accustomed to views across these lots had twice thwarted his attempts. His client wasn't inclined to try again.

To pay the design fees for the failed project, the client offered the lots, encumbered with a few thousand dollars in liens, to my friend. He didn't want to fight that battle himself, and he didn't have the money to pay the liens. If I would fight for the approvals and pay the liens, my friend would give me half of the land. My wife, Janet, a landscape architect, and I had long known that Santa Cruz would be our home for life. However, land here is so expensive that we were doubtful of ever finding an affordable building site. We borrowed the money and entered the fray.

After six rancorous public hearings and seven years of political and bureaucratic contentiousness, we at last obtained permits to build our home.

I prepared the sketchiest drawings that the city would accept before permitting the job. Then I designed on-site. Bill Schultz, who remains my best friend, built the house and guided me around the pitfalls of general contracting. The integrity, discipline, and spirit he brought to the project permeate the house. I was there at the beginning, middle, and end of each day, being apprised of upcoming issues and weighing advice given by seasoned, committed tradespeople. I delivered the details necessary to keep the next day's work on course and labored until dark and through weekends. It was the most productive and rewarding enterprise that I have ever undertaken.

Angled window bay lights the living room. The blood-red ceiling complements the plaster walls and helps to define the living room as a separate space. Photo taken at A on floor plan.

RIGHT Path of recycled bricks leads to the front door. The house's exterior is planned as a backdrop for gardens. For example, the sunlit west wall will eventually support espaliered fruit trees. Photo taken at B on floor plan.

BELOW Terrace off the master bedroom doubles as a sleeping porch. Most times, though, it's a quiet spot to sit and enjoy glimpses of Monterey Bay. Photo taken at E on floor plan.

FACING PAGE With only a little imagination, the house's facade resembles a face. On the practical side, the stucco finish was chosen to resist California's occasional wildfires. Photo taken at F on floor plan.

All architecture seeks to balance the public with the private, the spacious with the intimate.

Ceiling or Floor Changes Delineate Rooms and Preserve Interior Views

All architecture seeks to balance the public with the private, the spacious with the intimate, in everyday shelter. Our house was no exception. We didn't want to feel confined in our house: We wanted the long view through (see floor plans p. 141), yet we wanted each space to be well defined. I accomplished this goal in various ways. Low cabinets and two steps down delineate the living room (see photo p. 134). Changes in ceiling and floor finishes separate the kitchen from the dining room. A freestanding bookshelf defines a library within the space of the entry.

Our site is narrow, dropping steeply into an arroyo on the north and east, and abutting the rear fences of neighbors to the west. A long driveway approaches the parking area from the south. Walking toward the house beneath interwoven plane trees, we pass a vine-enclosed courtyard to arrive at the front door (see photo above).

The exterior walls are stucco, chosen to reflect the Mediterranean quality of our climate. A gold-and-olive-colored cement wash tops the stucco, filling the inevitable cracks. I plan to renew the wash every few years, using a different color. As the washes wear and fade, they'll show the underlying hues of previous washes. The walls will age honestly—no faux (see photo facing page).

Steps signal the living-room border. Beyond, the library is a private eddy not far from the flow of family life. Photo taken at D on floor plan.

Color Enlivens Ordinary Materials

The plastered interior walls are troweled smooth. Between six and nine pigments tint the plaster, depending on the color. By contrast, most commercial paints contain two or three pigments. This mix of pigments allows the walls to change hue as the lighting conditions vary through the day. The wood ceilings, sprayed red with a metal-based dye (U.S. Cellulose), are reminiscent

of oxblood-stained vaults of medieval Europe and complement the wall colors.

The deeply colored interior walls and ceilings create a solid, dug-in feel that takes the precariousness out of living on the edge of an arroyo. Two-story lightwells at both ends of the downstairs hall banish the gloom that can plague dark-walled spaces. The southern well is open and allows for conversation between the kitchen and the upstairs den. The northern well leads to the master bedroom and is capped with obscuring reed glass to deaden the sound.

Cliff Friedlander built the cabinets and bookcases from cherry. Some of the countertops in the kitchen and baths are granite (see photo left p. 140), culled from cutoffs at the local stone fabricator's shop. We followed our hearts for the main kitchen counter: hard rock maple finished with Behlen's Salad Bowl Finish from Mohawk Finishes (see Sources p. 140) (see photo above).

Floors in the library, dining room, upstairs den, entry, hall and stairway are of

ABOVE An antique stove begins the run of cabinets. Salad-bowl finish protects the rock-maple countertop. Photo taken at C on floor plan.

LEFT The screen in the cabinet door is left over from a confessional booth in a church designed by the author. Dividers in the plate rack below are simply ¼-in. cherry-veneer plywood. Photo taken at C on floor plan.

ABOVE **Protruding fir window frames negate any need for casings.** Providing a stop for the wall plaster, window frames were installed as the house was framed.

Window Frames That Need No Trim

Site-built 2-in.-thick Douglas-fir frames, dyed with metallic dyes that don't fade under sunlight (also from Mohawk Finishes), house the windows. Some frames protrude past the interior-wall plane by ¾ in., others by 4½ in., and they provide all the window trim we need (see photo above right). Frames for the dyed solid-core interior doors are treated in a similar way. Because the plaster butts to the window and door frames with no additional trim, we had to complete and varnish most of the finish carpentry during the rough framing.

The windows are either new powder-coated aluminum units intended for commercial use or steel units salvaged from a

ABOVE **Sink top of stone-yard scrap.** Originally the sink cut-out from someone else's kitchen counter, cast-off granite makes an elegant and inexpensive top.

SOURCES

U. S. Cellulose
(800) 683-8601

Mohawk Finishes
(800) 545-0047
www.mohawkfinishing.com

Forbo
(800) 842-7839
www.forbo.com

5-in.-wide cherry. The bathroom floors are 1-in. porcelain hexagonal tile that matches the 1930s moderne bath of our first family apartment. The kitchen and laundry have Forbo linoleum floors (see Sources). The bedrooms and living room are wool-carpeted, a more comfortable surface for bare feet and for sitting on.

1930s international-style building in Santa Cruz. I fought actively to save that building from demolition. After losing that fight, I was certain the building's owner wouldn't welcome me on the site, so a friend salvaged the windows for me. Brightly colored paint personalizes these otherwise utilitarian windows.

Recycled Materials Link New to Old

The house we built supports rather than masks who we are and what we hold dear. Every scrap of our controlled clutter represents some facet of our various community, family, and personal histories.

Sandstone steps from the old county jail, discarded as Santa Cruz rebuilt after the 1989 Loma Prieta earthquake, pave our entry. Janet and I spied them in a pile of debris behind a construction-site fence. The demolition contractor saved $300 in dumping fees by taking the steps to our site rather than to the city dump. Bricks from the former county courthouse, destroyed in the same earthquake, make up our hearth. An old friend's paintings on plywood comprise the panels of our dining-room cupboard doors.

I believe that you can and should judge domestic architecture by how well it supports a full and thoughtful life. I design homes for clients with the intent that after living there for a time, they will never want to leave.

We don't anticipate ever moving from our home. We own the lot next to ours, so our children may never need to move, either. The labor of construction is sweetest when you know that your children, and theirs, might enjoy its fruits.

Architect Mark Primack lives, practices, and is currently a city council member in Santa Cruz, California.

PLANNED AROUND THE SUN

The narrowness of the lot restricted the compass orientation of the house. Facing a broad wall to the sunny south wasn't possible. To compensate, two angled extensions reach out for the sun, and lightwells bring daylight to the inner recesses of the first floor.

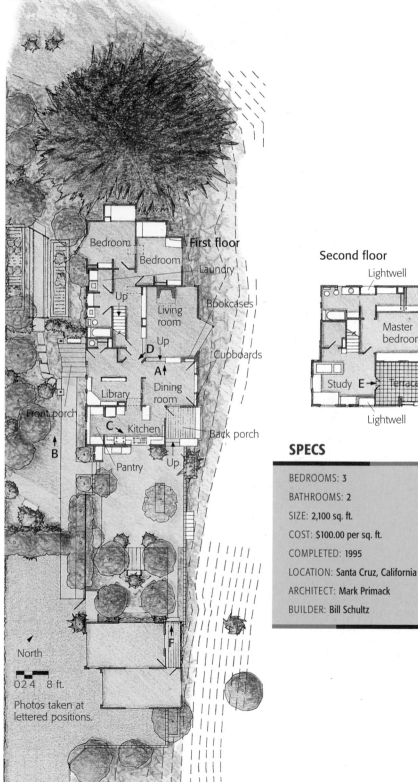

First floor

Bedroom
Bedroom
Laundry
Up
Living room
Bookcases
Up
D
Cubboards
A
Library
Dining room
Front porch
C
Kitchen
Back porch
B
Pantry
Up

Second floor

Lightwell
Master bedroom
Study E
Terrace
Lightwell

North

0 2 4 8 ft.

Photos taken at lettered positions.

F

SPECS

BEDROOMS: **3**

BATHROOMS: **2**

SIZE: **2,100 sq. ft.**

COST: **$100.00 per sq. ft.**

COMPLETED: **1995**

LOCATION: **Santa Cruz, California**

ARCHITECT: **Mark Primack**

BUILDER: **Bill Schultz**

Guest House by the Bay

A cozy old cabin on the river. Embedded corner boards and changing rooflines create the feeling of a little old house that never stopped growing. A balcony off the upstairs master bedroom takes in the view. Photo taken at A on floor plan.

S CATTERED ALONG THE NORTHERN FINGERS OF CHESAPEAKE Bay stands a collection of unlikely billboards. They are boathouses built long ago by highly skilled boatbuilders during the slow winter months. Rustic, even primitive, on the inside yet finely finished on the outside, these land-bound structures were calling cards, promoting their builders' skill and craftsmanship to anyone who happened to sail by. That's why it's not unusual to see highly creative trim elements that have been grafted to these otherwise modest structures.

Several years ago my clients bought an old Maryland dairy farm that included one of these dilapidated old boathouses. They hoped to resurrect the boathouse as a guest house, creating a comfortable place for his mother to stay during her frequent visits, but one that could also be used for large family gatherings. The old structure turned out to be too far gone to save. But its spirit, at least, was reborn in a new body.

Building an Old Boathouse

New construction in the Chesapeake Bay area is prohibited within 1,000 ft. of the waterline at mean high tide. We were permitted to build here because the guest house retained the footprint of the existing

RIGHT The warmest room in the house. Despite being part of the same great-room floor space that includes the two-story kitchen and dining areas, the area in front of the fireplace is a more intimate, comfortable space on a smaller scale. Photo taken at F on floor plan.

ABOVE **New uses for old stone.** The former stone foundation is now out of the ground, where it can be appreciated as the wall beneath the outdoor shower and as a new fireplace. Photo taken at H on floor plan.

boathouse. Beyond the uses they envisioned, they did not make specific demands for a particular style for Little Elk, as they named the guest house. Their only requirements were that the structure not dominate the view of the water from the main house up the hill and that it be sympathetic to its environment and its history.

The architecture of Maryland's Eastern Shore has traditionally reflected its connection to the water. Many of the ancient fishing cabins and boathouses that dot the shoreline have evolved significantly over the years. Oftentimes, families converted the boathouses to residential use, first adding a screened porch, later framing in that porch, then adding a new porch. These houses were my inspiration.

The rooflines and the exterior trim suggest an old house that never stopped growing (see photo pp. 142–143). Embedded corner boards extend up the gable-end walls to the point where the roof pitch changes, as if shed-roof additions had been grafted onto each side of a once-tiny house. The roof overhang stops at the "additions" to emphasize this effect. One of the porches is screened, one is open, and one is enclosed,

> *The architecture of Maryland's Eastern Shore has traditionally reflected its connection to the water.*

A COMFY YET EXPANSIVE RETREAT

Although primarily designed to be a cozy guest house for the owner's mother, this small cottage has an open floor plan and large screened porch that let it be the site of large family gatherings at the river.

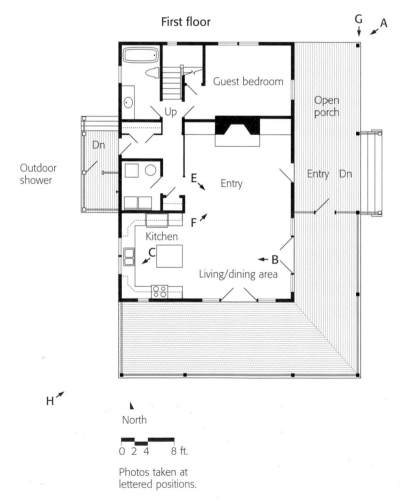

SPECS

BEDROOMS: 2

BATHROOMS: 2

SIZE: 1,674 sq. ft.

COST: n/a

COMPLETED: 1997

LOCATION: North East, Maryland

ARCHITECT: Peter Zimmerman Architects

BUILDER: Dan Burris (PHB Inc.)

Second floor

First floor

Photos taken at lettered positions.

implying that each of the house's porches was built at different times.

Historically, the building materials in this area of the country were primarily wood and brick—the brick arrived here as ballast in ships—but this tiny pocket of the Eastern Shore is one of the few areas where you see native stone. We salvaged the stone from the foundation of the old boathouse and used it to face the new foundation and to create the central fireplace (see photos pp. 144–145). Indoors and out, we used authentic, salvaged hardware from the late-19th century. All our hardware for the house came from the Michael M. Coldren Company in North East, Maryland (see Sources). Mike has one of the largest collections of 18th- and 19th-century hardware anywhere in the United States.

A Place for Every Season

Wraparound porches and oversize French doors allow Little Elk to expand for large parties and contract for warmth. In cold weather, with the doors closed, it's intimate and cozy, especially in front of a roaring fire in the stone fireplace. When it's time for the annual summer get-together, both sets of French doors in the dining area fold back on themselves, opening the walls onto the porches and letting in plenty of light and ventilation (see photo facing page). The porches are extra deep, which shields the interior spaces from the hot summer sun.

There's no drywall in the house because a boathouse that was converted to living space would have been roughly paneled with whatever material was at hand. To brighten the interior, the woodwork is finished with a light stain that allows the knots and natural grain to show through. The baseboards and casings are also finely planed knotty pine that's simply butted but subtly detailed with an occasional beaded edge.

An expansive space for entertaining. When the French doors that separate the dining area from the screened porch are open, the outside walls all but disappear. Photo taken at E on floor plan.

ABOVE A loft if you want it to be. Drawing back a 6-ft.-wide set of bifold shutters opens the south wall of the master bedroom onto the dining area below. Photo taken at D on floor plan.

There's no drywall in the house because a boathouse that was converted to living space would have been roughly paneled with whatever material was at hand.

ABOVE Indoor/outdoor dining. Alternative dining spaces flank the alcove kitchen. Photo taken at B on floor plan.

Deep screened porches could make a house feel dark and gloomy inside, so the upper-level windows are designed to funnel sunlight deep into the house. The loftlike master bedroom on the second floor has bifold shutters that open onto the dining area below or close for privacy (see top photo facing page). The master bedroom also has a private balcony, with French doors that open the wall to a view of sky and water (see photo p. 142).

The Fun Is in the Details

Throughout the planning, we never forgot that the guest house is a place for holidays, parties and fun. As a show of respect for our boat-building predecessors, I threw in a few whimsical details for guests to discover.

Everyone's favorite detail is the rafter tails. My clients changed the farm's live-stock from dairy cows to thoroughbred race-horses, so it seemed appropriate to carve the exposed rafter tails to resemble horses stretching for the finish line (see photo bottom right).

Local visitors can't help but notice the Chinese Chippendale railing that surrounds the balcony of the master bedroom. This style is a local tradition that is found on older houses throughout this area.

The other feature that delights guests is the outdoor shower (see photo top p. 145). Equally suited for a summertime cool-down or a rinse after a dip in the river, the outdoor shower exemplifies the link between land and water that Little Elk represents.

Peter Zimmerman, AIA, NCARB, is an architect in Berwyn, Pennsylvania.

ABOVE Looking out over the pasture. A cook at work in the kitchen can watch the horses at play in the farm's lower pasture. Photo taken at C on floor plan.

ABOVE Stretching for the finish line. Showing respect both for the work of the farm and for the crafts-manship of an earlier time, the exposed rafter tails are carved in the shape of horses' heads. Photo taken at G on floor plan.

SOURCES

Michael M. Coldren Company, Inc.
100 Race St.
North East, MD 21901
(410) 287-2082
www.coldrencompany.com

Round Roof
in the City

S ANDY AND I HAD BEEN FRIENDS SINCE CHILDHOOD, SO IT
didn't surprise me three years ago when he told me he wanted to
build his own house. Having seen his father build a log home from
scratch with no building experience, Sandy decided to act as general contractor, despite working a full-time job. As an architect, I would help with
the design of the house.

Building new hadn't been the original plan. Sandy and his wife, Jenny,
had tried and failed to find an older house to renovate in Vancouver.
Eventually, they bought a tear-down house on a small lot in East
Vancouver, an area of modest postwar bungalows and not-so-modest new
spec houses. Part of this lot's appeal was the potential for spectacular
views of the city and the mountains of Vancouver's North Shore (see
photo p. 152).

**Not your average neighbor-
hood house.** The combination of
exterior materials—a stucco facade,
wood trim, and a copper roof—
make this house a stand-out.

Room with a view. Although the house next door blocks the views from the lower floors, most of Vancouver is visible from the master bedroom and its deck. Photo taken at A on floor plan.

The plan that developed enclosed about 1,900 sq. ft. of living space (see floor plans p. 156). Jenny, who practices traditional Chinese medicine, required an examination room and a waiting room with a separate entry at the ground floor. The spare bedroom is on the ground floor as well, and the living room, dining room and kitchen make up the second floor. The master bedroom fills the upper floor. A wide glass door to a small deck takes advantage of a 180-degree view of Vancouver.

The Charm of a Timber-Frame House without the Cost

All of us would have preferred to build a post-and-beam house. But the cost was prohibitive, and we were on a tight budget. As a compromise, we incorporated exposed, heavy timbers wherever possible into an otherwise economical stick-frame house. The timbers are most conspicuous on the main floor. There, the plan is open to make the relatively small space appear larger (see photo top right p. 154). A grid of heavy timber beams and posts defines the spaces and accentuates details such as the fireplace and skylights (see photo facing page).

While Sandy, Jenny and I all liked the idea of large timbers in the house, we weren't crazy about the idea of razing an old-growth forest to get them. We thought using salvaged wood might be a way around this, and Sandy scoured the city for salvaged lumber (see sidebar p. 154). The 8x12 and 8x16 beams, the 8x8 posts, the flooring, and much of the millwork are Douglas fir that came from an old warehouse that was being demolished. The Douglas-fir floor joists and roof joists came from a supplier

> *We deliberately set out to design and build a strong counterpoint to the vinyl-clad, fake-brick-veneer spec houses that made up most of the new homes in the neighborhood.*

Zoning and Views Shape the House

We deliberately set out to design and build a strong counterpoint to the vinyl-clad, fake-brick-veneer spec houses that made up most of the new homes in the neighborhood (see photo p. 151). The house on the next lot to the north blocked most first-floor or second-floor views, but Sandy and Jenny's lot sloped downward enough to allow views from an upper floor. Because of height restrictions imposed by local zoning laws, this upper floor would have to tuck into the roof.

For small lots, zoning laws essentially limit houses to 2½ stories, with the upper half-story centered on the house under the roof. I played around with models of different roof options, and a curved roof was the most appealing solution.

Maximizing natural light in an often-dreary climate. Skylights and corner windows bring daylight indoors in Vancouver's cool, damp climate. Photo taken at D on floor plan.

Recycled Timbers Frame the Interior

In lieu of bearing walls, heavy beams support the framing above. The lack of walls fosters an open feel that belies the house's small size.

ABOVE Open risers allow southern light into the living room. A corner window, 13 ft. in height, extends below the landing. Glass is sandblasted for privacy. Photo taken at B on floor plan.

ABOVE Reclaimed timbers delineate the spaces of an open plan. The Douglas-fir flooring is salvaged, too, and spent its former life as heavy joists in a now-demolished factory. Photo taken at C on floor plan.

LEFT Not your traditional timber-frame joinery. Powder-coated steel connectors take the place of mortise-and-tenon joints, saving money and adding style.

of used building materials. Even the stairs are made of salvaged timber (see left photo facing page).

Once on site, the beams and posts were planed and then finished with a single coat of water-based polyurethane. The floor is made of 2x14 planks, former factory joists that were planed, tongued, and grooved, then screwed and plugged in place. Everyone said that these flooring planks were too wide and would shrink unacceptably, particularly because they were going over a radiant-heat system. After one year, however, I am happy to report only minor cracks (⅛ in. or so) between the boards.

I had imagined the salvaged wood to be full of gouges and holes. But this wood was spectacular: tight-grained with almost no knots or blemishes. The quality of the wood set the tone for the rest of the house.

The Play of Wood, Stucco, and Copper Enlivens the Exterior

Stucco clads the lower levels of the house, and board-and-batten cedar sides the upper level. I chose two different siding materials simply because I like the traditional Japanese look of wood playing off stucco.

I chose the stucco color by seeing what worked and what didn't on other houses. When we had a small sample mixed up, almost everyone, including the stucco contractor, balked at how dark the green was. But once applied and seen in contrast to the wood siding and windows, the stucco looked perfect.

The roof is standing-seam copper, and the gutters, downspouts, and all flashings are copper as well. Initially, I had imagined using a less expensive Galvalume metal roof, but Sandy priced copper and discovered that it didn't cost as much as we thought. The custom copper roof cost

$22,000 (Canadian) as opposed to $15,000 for Galvalume.

The roof is framed with 2x10s that sit perpendicular to the two arched exterior bearing walls. The top plate of these walls is composed of four layers of ¾-in. plywood, bent to follow the radius of the curve. The additional cost of the roof was really in the extra labor of building the walls: Each stud and each piece of siding are different lengths.

Deep 42-in. overhangs at both ends of the curved roof shade the house from both the summer sun and the winter rain. The exposed, curved rafters at these overhangs are carried by wood beams, which are in

I had imagined the salvaged wood to be full of gouges and holes. But this wood was spectacular: tight-grained with almost no knots or blemishes.

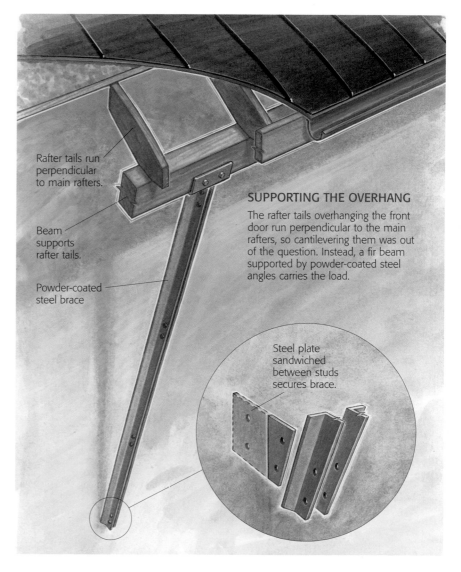

Rafter tails run perpendicular to main rafters.

Beam supports rafter tails.

Powder-coated steel brace

SUPPORTING THE OVERHANG

The rafter tails overhanging the front door run perpendicular to the main rafters, so cantilevering them was out of the question. Instead, a fir beam supported by powder-coated steel angles carries the load.

Steel plate sandwiched between studs secures brace.

PRIVACY INCREASES WITH HEIGHT

A hierarchy of privacy begins at the ground-floor medical clinic with its separate entry and culminates in the master bedroom on the upper floor. The main floor contains most of the living area in an open plan. Deliberately placed fir beams mark off the separate spaces of this floor.

SPECS

BEDROOMS: 2

BATHROOMS: 2 full, 2 half

SIZE: 1,900 sq. ft.

COST: n/a

COMPLETED: 2000

LOCATION: East Vancouver, British Columbia

ARCHITECT: Dan Parke

BUILDER: Sandy MacDonald

North

0 2 4   8 ft.

Photos taken at lettered positions.

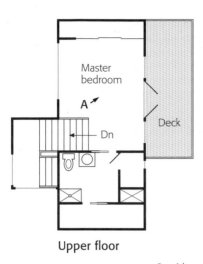

Upper floor

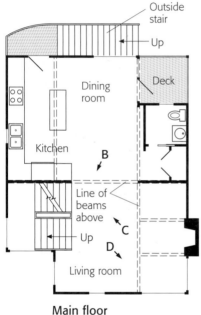

Main floor

Ground floor

turn carried by structural steel brackets, powder-coated for durability in Vancouver's damp climate (see drawing p. 155). This accent of steel carries through into the interior of the house: The post-and-beam connections and the angles supporting the stair treads are also powder-coated steel (see photo bottom p. 154).

The custom Douglas-fir windows are finished with two coats of Sikkens (see Sources) exterior penetrating stain. The window manufacturer, Mountainview Designs Ltd. (see Sources) had some difficulty finding long lengths of good-quality wood to use for the two 13-ft.-high windows at the stairs but came through in the end. The glass at the stair window is sandblasted to give some privacy; the effect is like a Japanese shoji screen.

The hydronic radiant-heating system is complemented by a heat-recovery ventilation system. The heat-distribution tubing on the lower level is in the slab on grade, and on the upper levels, the tubing runs in 1½ in. of concrete on top of the plywood decking. Due to space constraints, a decent-size mechanical room was sacrificed, and instead, the boiler is stuffed into a small space under the lowest stair landing. It was no fun for the mechanical contractor to install, but it works fine.

The Neighbors Take Notice

When the curved roof was being framed, it became clear that this residence was not going to be a normal house. The neighbors were surprisingly accepting, though. One exception was an anonymous person who expressed an opinion by taking potshots at the framers with a slingshot.

On the whole, though, the feedback has been positive. Jenny even once had a police officer come to the door, flash his badge, and then politely ask if he could take a look inside the house just out of curiosity.

The Ups and Downs of Salvaged Lumber

Using reclaimed wood has some definite pitfalls as well as distinct advantages. First, you have to find it, and there are a limited number of demolition contractors and salvagers. Once we knew the sizes of the timbers we needed, Sandy found a good source and bought what he hoped would be enough wood in the form of massive beams from an old factory. He trucked these beams 50 miles away to a small mill to be resawn into sizes we could use. Then the wood had to be graded, banded together, stickered, and kept out of rain and sun until it could be used. Months later, Sandy had it trucked back to his lot. Most contractors would roll their eyes at the thought of the additional time and hassle.

Be sure that you buy enough lumber, because if you're short, it's almost impossible to buy small quantities later on.

Some subtrades don't like to work with salvaged lumber because old lumber can be dry and hard, and it could have nails or other surprises hidden in it. Also, reclaimed wood shouldn't be mixed with new wood because the two likely will have different moisture contents and shrinkage potential.

The advantages include the fact that reclaimed wood is usually dry and much more stable and predictable than new wood. And there is the satisfaction of knowing the wood you are using has a history. Was the recycled wood we used in this house less expensive than buying new? No. Is it better? Absolutely.

One other thing: Unlike a typical job site where the lumber scraps are sent away in a Dumpster, Sandy saved all but the smallest. He's still making furniture out of his stash of leftovers. —D. P.

ABOVE Does your favorite lumberyard stock this size beam? **RIGHT** Salvaged from a now-razed warehouse, this 21-ft.-long, 13-in. by 29-in. Douglas-fir timber was resawn into beams for the house in this article.

To complete the circle, Sandy's father, who had retired recently, had time to help out on the house. He built the kitchen and bathroom cabinets, had a major hand in the interior finishing, and even made some furniture.

One change in use happened between the design stage and now. The spare bedroom is now the office for Sandy's construction company, which he was inspired to start after building this house.

Dan Parke is principal of his own firm, SaLaL Architecture, on Bowen Island, BC, Canada.

SOURCES

Sikkens
(800) 833-7288
www.sikkens.com

Mountainview Designs Ltd.
(604) 987-5630

Simple House,
Contemporary Look

WHY DO HOUSES LOOK AS IF THEY WERE DESIGNED AND built in a previous century, in contrast to cars or clothes, for example? As a designer, my own preferences lean toward modern and simple. However, I'm also a builder, and I appreciate the efficiency and construction logic behind many standard house-building

The author designed his parents' retirement home with simplicity and light in mind. Mix-and-match windows provide ample views of the lake.

techniques, as opposed to a lot of modern residential design, which I think is often too fussy in its detailing. In my own work, I've been trying to combine a modern use of form, color, material, light, and space with a builder's practical concern for efficiency and cost.

Design Doesn't Have to Be Fancy

My parents had been talking vaguely for years about building a retirement house, but I thought it was just talk. Then one day, they surprised me by saying they were ready to sell their house in Winnipeg, Manitoba, and asking me to build them a retirement house outside the city. At the time, I'd been a partner in a small design/build company based in Toronto, doing mostly residential and commercial renovations and additions. The idea of

I've been trying to combine a modern use of form, color, material, light, and space with a builder's practical concern for efficiency and cost.

taking a break from the big city appealed to me, so I decided to go home and build a place for my parents.

They'd decided to retire to a small town on the west shore of Lake Winnipeg, a vast lake in the middle of the Canadian prairie. We found a pie-shaped lot just outside town with a 60-ft. frontage on the road and a 300-ft. beach frontage on the lake.

Although the lot was low (it had been half-covered with a foot of water in the spring), that long beach frontage was tempting. After several days of fretting and considering, they bought the lot.

To my surprise, I discovered that my parents, longtime owners of a traditional suburban house, also shared many of my ideas about design. We all wanted the house to feel open, transparent to the prairie sky, the land, and the amazing lake. They particularly liked the idea of simple forms, high ceilings, and lots of light, so these three

things became the basic principles of the design. I also wanted to take advantage of the width of the site (150 ft. at the closest point to the water defined by the setback) by making the house long and narrow. This linear plan would allow every room to have a view of the lake and also a view toward the road and the southwest, which receives most of the light. Most important, everyone agreed that the house had to be reasonably priced.

Simple Layout for Light and Views

The final design of 1,950 sq. ft. consists of two small rectangular buildings with shed roofs, connected by an enclosed bridge. I figured that two buildings would break up the mass of a long narrow building and would look less like a job-site trailer. Building One, 20 ft. wide by 50 ft. long,

contains an entry area, a great room that combines living, dining and kitchen areas, and a laundry/storage room. Building Two, which is 18 ft. wide and 44 ft. long and slightly skewed in relation to the first building, contains two bedrooms, two baths, and a tower room that functions as an office/guest bedroom with a great lofty view. A large dormer/skylight over the kitchen balances the elevation and brings in lots of light during the afternoon. During the design process, I tried a variety of dormer and skylight combinations, but I liked this one the best.

Because the mosquito is Manitoba's unofficial provincial bird, there are two screened porches (see photo below), one that faces the lake off the living/kitchen area and a smaller one off the master bedroom. There's also an open deck off the large screened porch, and a covered but unscreened porch running the length of the front side of Building One. This front porch is a good place to watch the sunset and the cars going by, and it also provides shade from the strong southwest summer sun. The second-story tower room also has a deck; although small, the deck affords the best views of the lake.

Pilings Keep the House Afloat on a Sea of Unstable Clay

I planned to do most of the construction myself; in August, I began by subbing out the foundation to a local contractor. In this part of Manitoba, the soil is heavy, water-saturated, unstable clay, locally referred to as gumbo. Instead of basements with foundation walls on perimeter strip footings, the typical foundation is a concrete grade beam

This linear plan would allow every room to have a view of the lake and also a view toward the road and the southwest, which receives most of the light.

Screened porches offer protected views. In summer, asylum from sun and mosquitoes is at each end of the house. Photo taken at C on floor plan.

Assembling a jigsaw of smaller windows for a larger view. Built into a frame of 2x6s, this asymmetrical combination of fixed and casement windows makes use of individual units that were discounted seconds. Photo taken at B on floor plan.

supported by piles. Big piles. In our case, we poured 16-in.-dia. concrete piles that were sunk down 20 ft. and spaced 10 ft. apart. A concrete grade beam 8 in. wide by 24 in. high spans the piles and carries the weight of the house. We also used the same-size piles for all the porches. The holes for the piles were filled with concrete as soon as possible after they were drilled to prevent them from filling with water, which can make for an unstable pile. The foundation contractor had the concrete trucks arriving and filling up the holes before the drilling rig was even finished drilling the last of them.

I worked with the foundation crew forming and pouring the grade beams, which we

started several days after the piles were sufficiently cured. It took us only a day and a half to form the grade beams for both buildings. We poured the concrete the following morning and stripped forms three days later. I now had a good level foundation ready for framing.

I had about two months, maybe a little longer, before the cold and snow of a Manitoba winter would arrive, and I wanted to have the house framed and enclosed before then. I'd hired a helper just out of high school, Ryan Peterson, and we put in long six-day weeks for the next two months, framing, sheathing, and shingling. We finished the roof one day before the first snow in November.

I used metal studs for all the interior non-load-bearing walls because they're light and easy to work with, especially in a situation where the ceilings are sloping and every stud is a different height. I'd learned the advantages of metal studs in commercial interior renovation work, where ceilings and floors often dip and bow and where precision-cutting wood studs and toenailing them from a ladder is a real pain. There's still a bias against metal studs in residential work, but I like them fine.

For some of the large windows, we saved money by buying a bunch of new double-insulated windows that had been made the wrong size. I designed these windows based on the different sizes of units, fitting them together like a jigsaw puzzle (see photo left). We made the jambs and heads out of 2x6 #2 pine and captured the glass between ¾-in. stops; we used 2x8s for the sills.

Although a lot of extra labor was required, I figure we saved several thousand dollars in materials costs on these windows over the cost of manufactured windows. If I had been charging my usual rates for my time, it probably would have come out about even.

Instead of a linear plan resembling an office trailer, the author designed two separate buildings and connected them with an elevated bridge. Each room has wide-angle views of the lake and prairie; as a result, the house seems more transparent. A second-story office/guest room balances the long horizontal exterior.

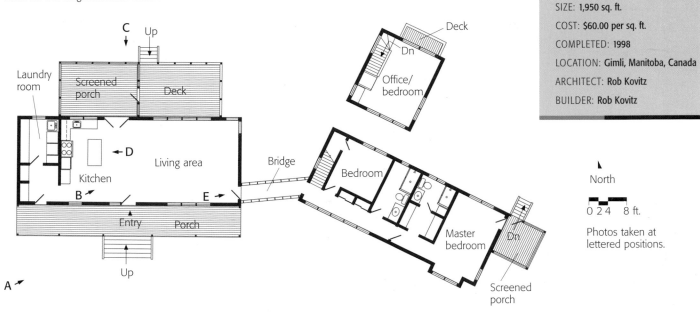

SPECS

BEDROOMS: **3**

BATHROOMS: **2**

SIZE: **1,950 sq. ft.**

COST: **$60.00 per sq. ft.**

COMPLETED: **1998**

LOCATION: **Gimli, Manitoba, Canada**

ARCHITECT: **Rob Kovitz**

BUILDER: **Rob Kovitz**

North

0 2 4   8 ft.

Photos taken at lettered positions.

Metal Siding: Colorful and Inexpensive

It had warmed up by the time we finished hanging drywall in late April, so I subbed out the taping and moved outside to work on the metal siding. We chose a corrugated-steel siding with a custom red finish that cost us a 10% premium over the standard eight colors available. Steel siding is fairly inexpensive if detailed simply, about 55¢ per sq. ft. for plain galvanized and 75¢ per sq. ft. for prepainted. Flashing and trims added another 25¢ per sq. ft. to the cost. It's not as cheap as vinyl siding, but much less than wood clapboards, both of which we had also considered. Steel is also durable and easy to maintain. I might have used vinyl if it came in richer, brighter colors, but it doesn't; the colors fade in the sun. Vinyl also feels very cheap to the touch. For accent, I used bright galvanized siding on the bridge, bedroom bay window, kitchen skylight, and roof flashing.

Installation is fairly simple. We first installed the flashing at the tops and bottoms of walls and around window/door openings. The sheets can be ordered precut to the exact length, but the openings still have to be cut. We cut the sheets face down with a circular saw to avoid marring the finish; face protection and long-sleeve shirts are a must. The sheets were then screwed every 12 in. to the sheathing with the supplied screws and neoprene washers.

Interior Is Spare and Spacious

The house's interior finishes are generally simple and inexpensive; the large volumes and prairie light provide all the decoration needed. For instance, I used precut medium-density fiberboard (MDF) for the baseboards and door trim, 4½ in. and 2½ in. wide respectively, and painted them the same white as the walls. The windows are finished without trim except for the sills and

I'd learned the advantages of metal studs in commercial interior renovation work, where ceilings and floors often dip and bow.

High ceilings and lots of light are important. Illuminated by a large skylight and utilitarian ceiling fixtures, the kitchen area is cooled by ample cross ventilation. Photo taken at D on floor plan.

aprons; the drywall is returned into vinyl J-trim that was ordered with the windows. This gives them a clean, uncluttered look, like an industrial window in a studio loft.

I carried the industrial theme further with galvanized light fixtures, which cost about $8 each. In the kitchen (see photo above). I rigged up hanging lights from the same fixtures, some octagonal boxes, standard ½-in. electrical conduit, and a few couplings. For the flooring, I used dark-green vinyl tile with a texture meant to resemble slate; it's inexpensive, easy to install, and easy to maintain.

I put in a few special touches. To spruce up the stairs leading to the office, I used clear-finished Baltic-birch plywood fastened with round-head screws; the treads are covered with the same vinyl tile I used everywhere else. I left the studs exposed between the bridge's windows (see photo right). Cutting and fastening the framing had to be precise. The bare wood makes a warm contrast to the red painted ceiling and white walls.

A local manufacturer made the cabinets of maple plywood finished in a clear gloss lacquer. At my mother's request, the counters are 38 in. high, 2 in. higher than standard; the red laminate closely matches the red siding. A local HVAC contractor used anodized aluminum and exposed rivets to make a great-looking range hood at about 20% of the cost of a hood from a fancy kitchen store.

Climate Control Doesn't Have to be Complicated

Because we had cross-ventilation in every room and a pretty constant breeze that blows off the lake, we installed ceiling fans in every room instead of air conditioning. The combination of fans, wide porch roofs, and cotton roll-up blinds keeps the house cool on even the hottest days. To heat the house, we installed electric baseboard units (there was no gas available in the area). Because electric baseboards don't require ductwork, they're also inexpensive to install and easily controlled on a room-by-room basis.

I insulated the structure with code-standard R-21 fiberglass batts in the 2x6 walls, R-38 in the 14-in.-deep plywood joist roofs, and a heated crawlspace that's protected with rigid insulation. I probably should have gone for some extra insulation, considering how much exterior volume there is for the amount of floor area, and because electric heating, whether furnace or base-

A well-lighted passageway. The connecting bridge is lined with windows that flood the interior with light. Photo taken at E on floor plan.

board, is more expensive to run than gas. But since the house was built, a new gas line has been run through the area, and my parents are considering switching to a gas furnace, which should decrease the heating bill somewhat.

_____

Rob Kovitz is an architect/builder in Winnipeg, Manitoba, Canada.

A Cozy Vermont House

W HEN VISITORS TOUR OUR SMALL HOUSE FOR THE FIRST time, I can now predict the oohs and aahs. Everyone seems to be enchanted by the same details: the intimate breakfast nook, the large windows with great views, the warm red bathroom with a big tub, the staircase that recalls the Craftsman era. For my partner, Jim Kirby, and me, the details represent the house as a whole: a carefully planned project that yielded wonderful results.

By necessity, economy was at the top of our list, so we had to design and build a large portion of the house ourselves. Tom Meyer of Progressive Home Builders in Putney, Vermont, handled the framing, insulation, drywall, and interior trim; we did everything else. As the house progressed, we worked to make the pleasing details more economically feasible. The cumulative result of these details has proved to be greater than each feature's cost, as we discovered when the house was recently assessed at 23% more than our cost to build it. Combined with the house's energy efficiency, these details make life in this modest house a real joy.

Cozy living room. Rich wood detailing and varied ceiling heights make this living room warm and inviting. Photo taken at A on floor plan.

HOUSE WARM

The house was built to be as energy efficient as possible during long Vermont winters. The key elements included R-40 insulation in the rafters, double-insulated exterior walls, radiant heating, and an insulated foundation.

R-40 fiberglass batts in rafters

Poly vapor barrier

½-in. rigid insulation taped at the seams

Argon-filled, low-e glass

Exterior walls have an R-factor of 27.8

Builder Tom Meyer created this warmer wall by nailing rigid insulation to the studs inside and sealing the joints. Horizontal 2x4s nailed on 18-in. centers provided backing for the drywall and made a handy chase for wiring.

2x4s

R-19 fiberglass batts

2x6 framing

Caulked at floor and ceiling

Radiant-floor tubing

Rigid insulation

Drywall

6-in. fiberglass batts

Reflective rigid insulation reflects heat upward

Radiant heat was installed in the first- and second-floor joists, as well as in the basement slab. Rigid insulation below the tubing increases the system's efficiency. Insulated foundation walls raise the house's overall R-value.

Poly vapor barrier

Creative Framing Increases R-Value

Here in Vermont, the winters are long and cold; summer seems fleeting. To offset the high costs of heating, we wanted the house to be as well insulated as possible and liked what Tom Meyer had done in the past with other projects. Over the course of 20 or 30 houses, Tom had personalized a method of wall framing that beefed up the walls' insulation. He framed the walls with 2x6s, insulated the bays with R-19 fiberglass, then nailed ½-in. rigid insulation onto the inside of the studs, sealing the joints with caulk at ceilings and floors, and sealing vertical seams with packing tape. Next, he air-nailed 2x4s horizontally on 18-in. centers. He used the spaces between the horizontals as wiring chases; insulated staples kept the wires safely away from drywall screws. When the drywall was installed, the resulting airspace added extra R-value to the wall, creating an R-value of 27.8. To keep the house tight, we also had the roof insulated with fiberglass batts to an R-value of 40.

Radiant Heat Is Clean

We chose to heat the house with a hydronic radiant-floor system because of its even heat distribution and because it is clean. Both of us have respiratory problems; unlike forced-hot-air or baseboard systems, radiant heat doesn't collect dust or blow it into the air. It is also delightful to step onto a warm bathroom floor on a cold winter morning.

The system is fired by a Thermo-Dynamics oil-burner that's efficient and costs about $600 less than comparable units from other manufacturers (see Sources p. 173). We installed the system ourselves; Jim had a fair amount of experience as a heating contractor and knew the basics. I had less experience but found the whole process to be relatively uncomplicated. We laid the tubing in the basement slab and ran the first- and second-floor tubing between the floor joists, insulating the joist cavities afterward with reflective rigid insulation to direct the heat upward.

Our home is in a 7,400 heating degree-day climate, compared with the national average of about 5,000 degree-days. We heat the home for about 18¢ per sq. ft. of living area, or 3.4 Btus per sq. ft. per degree-day. We use 550 gal. of fuel oil annually; at 80¢ per gallon, the heating cost is $440 a year. Unlike many Vermonters, we don't supplement our heat with wood. On occasion, we do have a fire in the fireplace, but it's mostly for looks.

Windows Add to Energy Efficiency

When choosing windows for this house, we not only considered the factors of light and ventilation, but also heat gain and the windows' location in the house. Facing south, our site offers extraordinary short-range views that include fields, a white-pine forest, beaver ponds, and a ridgeline;

To offset the high costs of heating, we wanted the house to be as well-insulated as possible.

Energy-efficient windows increase the house's appeal. A casement window lights the large tub (see photo top right taken at E on floor plan) and increases solar gain; a large slider provides a great view from the bedroom (see photo bottom right taken at F on floor plan).

LEFT By combining good design sense and sweat equity, the author and her family built a relatively inexpensive house that's both gracious and warm. Photo taken at B on floor plan.

SMALL ON THE OUTSIDE, BIGGER ON THE INSIDE

Modest in size, the house's interior seems much larger due to the one-story wing that forms the central space of the living/dining room. In addition, large windows in key locations open up each of the rooms.

SPECS

BEDROOMS: 2

BATHROOMS: 2

SIZE: 1,686 sq. ft., not including basement and attic

COST: $159.00 per sq. ft., including land ($39,500) and site costs ($21,000); does not include owner's considerable sweat equity

COMPLETED: 1996

LOCATION: Brookline, Vermont

ARCHITECT: Leslie Hill

BUILDERS: Leslie Hill/Jim Kirby

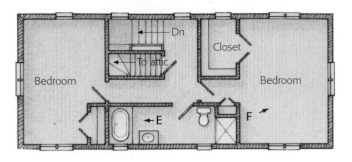

Second floor

North

0 2 4   8 ft.

Photos taken at lettered positions.

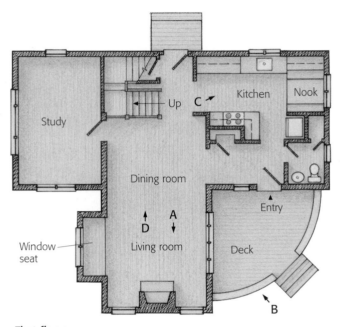

First floor

---

we needed to see as much of this scenery as possible.

With this much glazing planned, we searched for an economical, energy-efficient window and found that Lincoln Windows manufactured a unit designed for northern applications (see Sources p. 173). We chose R-4 windows (R-9 units were too expensive) that are argon-filled, are double-glazed, and have a hard, low-e coating designed to optimize passive-solar gain. Using an estimating program called Energy-10 (available from the Passive Solar Industries Council), Jim calculated that 120 sq. ft. of windows on the south side of the house would gain more heat than the rest of the house's windows lose. The windows on the east, west,

and north represent only about 12% of the overall heat loss from the house, but this amount is more than offset by the solar gain from the south windows. On sunny winter days, the combination of these efficient windows and a well-insulated envelope keeps the house up to temperature and our fuel bills lower.

We discovered that sliding wooden windows manufactured by Lincoln for the condominium replacement market cost 15% to 20% less than double-hung or casement windows, so we incorporated sliders into the design and ganged them to achieve wide, tall windows. We also used a few casements for design contrast.

A staircase can be functional art. Built on a tight budget, the yellow-pine risers and treads and fir railing still lend a warm, stately glow to the living room. A small window at the landing casts light into the house's interior. Photo taken at D on floor plan.

Stairs Should Be Elegant

If designed and built with care, a staircase can be a dominant piece of functional art inside a house. With the Craftsman style in mind, I specified an open stringer and designed a simple geometric railing. To stay within budget, we chose yellow-pine treads and risers and a fir railing. Tom Meyer insisted on making the stairs wider than I had requested, and he was right. These stairs (see photo above) nearly 4 ft. wide,

make it easy to move the variety of things that travel from floor to floor. Located on an outside wall, a narrow window on the staircase landing throws natural light into the dining room below.

At the top of the stairs, a narrow door that appears to be a linen closet opens to reveal stairs to the attic. Modern houses are usually designed with flimsy fold down attic stairs, but permanent stairs make the job of storage easier. There is also nothing like a dry, roomy, convenient attic for keeping a

If designed and built with care, a staircase can be a dominant piece of functional art inside a house.

Breakfast nook is the heart of the kitchen. Inspired by a kitchen from the author's childhood, this intimate area provides a secluded space for meals beneath a large window. Bench seats conceal extra storage. Photo taken at C on floor plan.

house organized. Naturally, we have a window in our attic, too, for added light.

In the Kitchen, a Nook Creates a Contrast of Space

Recently, some visiting children entered the kitchen, turned to their mother and exclaimed, "Look! It's just like a restaurant!" That must be how I felt as a child and why I

brought this dinerlike kitchen table into my daily life. For one end of the galley kitchen, I designed a cozy breakfast nook (see photo above) with built-in benches that have hidden storage. The inspiration for this design came right out of a 1920s house from my childhood. A breakfast/supper nook is an intimate area, conducive to conversation and quiet meals. A wide window over the table opens onto a view of the side yard and

SOURCES

Thermo-Dynamics
Route 61, Box 325
Schuylkill Haven, PA 17972
(717) 385-0731

Lincoln Wood Products Inc.
701 N. State St., P. O. Box 375
Merrill, WI 54452
(715) 536-2461

Passive Solar Industries Council
(202) 628-7400
www.psic.org

garden. The benches are 5 ft. long and 18 in. deep, and they seat four comfortably and six in a pinch.

In the living room, a window seat (see photo p. 166) offers a view of the pond in back and is a great spot for morning coffee, a novel, or a nap. The ceiling above it is dropped and has two recessed lights set on a dimmer switch. Built of fir, the window seat has enough storage space beneath its hinged lid for Christmas decorations, puzzles, games, photo albums, and gift wrap.

Leslie Hill enjoys a lifelong interest in residential design and construction. She works at Harvard University.

Part Office, Mostly House

I F I WERE SUPERSTITIOUS, I WOULD BELIEVE THAT OCTOBER IS A bad month for me. In October 1989, California was hit by the Loma Prieto earthquake. My business, a 108-room hotel in Oakland, California, was seriously damaged. After two years of negotiation and some hefty repair bills, my partners and I sold it.

From that sale, I bought what I call The Ranch: about an acre of land and six buildings in West Oakland, a part of the city that had fallen on hard times. The deal included some sheds, a barn, and the Duck Kee Market, featured on a Creedence Clearwater Revival album cover. The buildings were marginal at best. It was a mess, but a promising mess. Out of the hotel business, I decided to return to my earlier career as a developer. My plan was to fix up the houses and rent them to artists.

Breaking the house into two parts. Separating the living portion of the house, on the right, from the office/apartment, on the left, allows daylight easy access to every room. Photo taken at B on floor plan.

The live part of live/work. The kitchen range-counter overlooks the sitting and dining areas. In the distance, the office lies beyond the courtyard. Photo taken at C on floor plan.

Two Years Later

Then, in October 1991, a fire storm hit the Oakland Hills. My home and all that it held were reduced to ash by 2:30 in the afternoon. I was lucky to escape with my life. Looking back on it, I was in shock for several years. The smell of smoke will always scare me. But I had this collection of run-down houses in West Oakland that needed fixing, and I was too busy to grieve much for my house and my departed art collection. I stayed with friends for a few days. Then a business colleague called and said he had a huge empty building not far from The Ranch. Would I care to live there for a couple of months in one of the vacant studios? I gratefully accepted, and a new chapter began.

This was the first time I had lived in a warehouse/loft. It was exciting. The neighborhood was gritty, but the people were nice. I made some new friends and got used to new household patterns. I didn't have much stuff. Everything was new.

About a year after the fire, I drove up to the hill one Sunday afternoon. I hadn't been there for months. To my horror, the houses that had been framed adjacent to

DIVIDE THE HOUSE, CONQUER THE PROBLEM

If you're going to live and work at home, it's nice to have some physical and psychological separation between the two. To that end, this house consists of two parts. The west wing includes the garage and the office, with a guest apartment upstairs. The east wing is the main house.

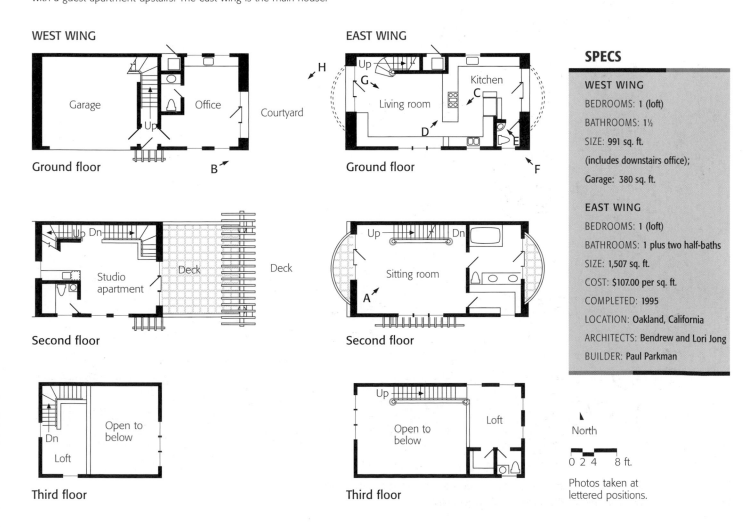

WEST WING

Ground floor — Garage, Office, Courtyard

Second floor — Studio apartment, Deck, Deck

Third floor — Loft, Open to below

EAST WING

Ground floor — Living room, Kitchen

Second floor — Sitting room

Third floor — Open to below, Loft

SPECS

WEST WING
BEDROOMS: 1 (loft)
BATHROOMS: 1½
SIZE: 991 sq. ft.
(includes downstairs office);
Garage: 380 sq. ft.

EAST WING
BEDROOMS: 1 (loft)
BATHROOMS: 1 plus two half-baths
SIZE: 1,507 sq. ft.
COST: $107.00 per sq. ft.
COMPLETED: 1995
LOCATION: Oakland, California
ARCHITECTS: Bendrew and Lori Jong
BUILDER: Paul Parkman

North

0 2 4   8 ft.

Photos taken at lettered positions.

and across the street from my lot were four times the size they had been in their previous lives. It was disgusting. I drove back down the hill and put my lot up for sale.

A couple more months went by, and ideas floated around in my head about where I was going to live. To build or not to build? Because I am in the building business, building anew seemed like a reasonable thing to do. But where? I looked at lots all over the Bay Area. And then I started looking at The Ranch from a different perspective. It looked like West Oakland was beginning to take a turn for the better, and The Ranch had a nice empty corner that needed a house.

Industrial Tuscan. Battered walls and metal detailing forge an eclectic, stylistic mix that's right at home in its light-industrial neighborhood. At the roofline, the corrugated-steel cornice incorporates the rain-gutter system. It's punctuated at the corners by spun-aluminum flagpole balls. Photo taken at F on floor plan.

ABOVE A peninsula screens the cooktop. A raised counter topped with a rusty-red slab of marble divides the living space from the kitchen. Stainless-steel appliances contrast with terra-cotta-colored tiles. Photo taken at D on floor plan.

ABOVE Upstairs in the east wing. A two-story-tall space on the second floor holds a sitting room and a big bathroom with a generous tub. Photo taken at A on floor plan.

Two Simple Buildings Equal One House, an Office, and an Apartment

The lot is long and narrow, and runs east to west. There are simple Victorians on one side, a two-story flat-roofed building on the other, and industrial buildings across the street. I studied rooflines, took photos, and considered options. Flat roofs seemed to fit.

My idea was to use industrial materials and lots of color (see photo facing page). I did not have a lot of money to work with, but I wanted to do something that had style. The house would have a great big kitchen (see photo top left). And it needed lots of light, lots of bathrooms, an office for my work and guest quarters. I wanted a quiet room for sitting, with a loft above it for my bed (see photo top right). Finally, I wanted a courtyard that would serve as an outdoor living and dining room (see photo right).

The idea of splitting the house into two buildings came from the architects, Bendrew and Lori Jong. Lori had the idea to cant the

ABOVE A short commute across the patio. Facing south, the court-yard between the house and the office/apartment is sheltered from the westerly winds and open to the sun. Photo taken at H on floor plan.

exterior walls to create structural interest with minimal extra expense. The contractor, Paul Parkman, thought of the grand, corrugated-metal cornice/roof cap. This clever detail also carries the roof-drain system and puts a distinctive lid on the house.

Fun with Color

The concrete floors were my project. First, I tried painting the concrete floors with a concrete paint in a sort of maroon color. It looked dreadful, sucked up all the light and was extremely flat. So one weekend, in a fit of hating the way the floors looked, I got out my little hand sanders and started sanding off the paint. I experimented with various grits, leaving some paint on the floor. And the thing just evolved. I started out to remove all evidence of the nasty flat maroon color and ended up with a sort of striated maroon floor (see photo below). Then polish, lots of polish. I like polishing the floors—I remember my Great Aunt Isabel when I polish. She maintained that it took years (like 30) to polish tile floors properly. To get the patina, she mixed crankcase oil and turpentine: It gave the house a special smell for a couple of days. But her tile floors were a thing of beauty.

The rest of the kitchen. On the right, the prep sink overlooks the kitchen garden on the south side of the house. Mottled maroon concrete floors run throughout this ground-floor level. Photo taken at G on floor plan.

Pattern and color enhance a half-bath. Pinstriped patterns of light play across an unexpected color scheme in the downstairs bathroom. Photo taken at E on floor plan.

This building was conceived as a sculptural block against which landscaping would stand. Multiple trellises sprout from the walls and perch above columns awaiting bougainvillea vines (see photo p. 175). I chose a cinnamon-colored stucco for the exterior. It's a warm color that makes a good foil for the plants. The overpowering colors are inside, in small doses for a little variety, such as the red, green and blue in the downstairs bathroom (see photo above).

The Humiliation of Creation

That's what I call it. You learn something every time you build. The house is not perfect; houses never are. Next time, I'll do open shelving in the corner kitchen cabinets. I've got those lazy Susan turntables in there now, and they just don't work for me. The painted medium-density fiberboard cabinet doors were also a mistake. Their edges tend to get chipped; then the material

starts to swell. Next time, I'll use solid wood. Even though they're up to code, the stairways are too narrow. They work fine. I have just decided I like wider stairways. And next time, I'll put more closets in the bathrooms and pay closer attention to their lighting.

The garage has seen my car once, maybe. That tells me I need a workshop/storage/staging area. The garage has become that place. The old Jag lives outside. Someday, I'll give up some yard space for a garage. On the other hand, the office space is great. I love being able to come over here in the early morning or late at night and work quietly. I like being able to say, "Hey, let's go across the patio and cook lunch." We do that a lot.

Kathryn Porter is a ceramic artist and a developer living in Oakland, California.

Credits

The articles compiled in this book appeared in the following issues of *Fine Homebuilding*:

p. iii: Photo by Charles Miller, courtesy *Fine Homebuilding*, © The Taunton Press, Inc.

p. v: Photo by Andy Engel, courtesy *Fine Homebuilding*, © The Taunton Press, Inc.

Table of Contents: p. vi (top to bottom)—photos by Roe A. Osborn, Scott Gibson, Charles Miller, David Ericson, and Charles Miller, courtesy *Fine Homebuilding*, © The Taunton Press, Inc. p. 1 (top to bottom)—photos by Charles Bickford, courtesy *Fine Homebuilding*, © The Taunton Press, Inc.,© Bruce Kelley, ©Brian Vanden Brink, Tom O'Brien, Charles Miller, courtesy *Fine Homebuilding*, © The Taunton Press, Inc.

p. 2: Photo by Andy Engel, courtesy *Fine Homebuilding*, © The Taunton Press, Inc.

p. 4: When Builder Weds Architect by Mike Guertin, issue 123. All photos by Roe A. Osborn, courtesy *Fine Homebuilding*, © The Taunton Press, Inc. Drawings by Scott Bricher, © The Taunton Press, Inc.

p. 12: Downsizing with Style by David O'Neil, issue 132. All photos by Roe A. Osborn, courtesy *Fine Homebuilding*, © The Taunton Press, Inc. Drawings by Mark Hannon, © The Taunton Press, Inc.

p. 22: A Basic Box Isn't All Bad by Kelly Davis, issue 126. All photos by Roe A. Osborn, courtesy *Fine Homebuilding*, © The Taunton Press, Inc. Drawings by Dan Thornton, © The Taunton Press, Inc.

p. 30: In the Belly of the Barn by Brian Reading, issue 139. All photos by Tom O'Brien, courtesy *Fine Homebuilding*, © The Taunton Press, Inc., except photos pp. 34, 36 © Brian Reading. Drawings by Ron Carboni, © The Taunton Press, Inc.

p. 38: A Rustic Country Cottage by David Edrington, issue 121. All photos by Charles Miller, courtesy *Fine Homebuilding*, © The Taunton Press, Inc. Drawings p. 43 by Mark Hannon, © The Taunton Press, Inc. Drawings pp. 44, 45 by Vince Babak, © The Taunton Press, Inc.

p. 46: A House Designed by Consensus by Scott Gibson, issue 122. All photos by Scott Gibson, courtesy *Fine Homebuilding*, © The Taunton Press, Inc. Drawings p. 49 by Dan Thornton, © The Taunton Press, Inc. Illustration p. 50 © Cline Davis Architects.

p. 52: Building Smaller, for Now by Robert Knight, issue 141. Photos pp. 53, 55 © Robert Perron. Photos pp. 57, 58, 59 by Tom O'Brien, courtesy *Fine Homebuilding*, © The Taunton Press, Inc. All drawings by Ron Carboni, © The Taunton Press, Inc.

p. 62: An Industrial Loft in Texas by Richard Wintersole, issue 144. Photos pp. 62, 66 (top), 67 by David Ericson, courtesy *Fine Homebuilding*, © The Taunton Press, Inc. Photos pp. 63, 66 (bottom) © Mike Bodycomb. Photos p. 64 © Richard Wintersole. Drawings by Ron Carboni, © The Taunton Press, Inc.

p. 68: A House Disguised as a Cottage by William F. Roslansky, issue 129. All photos by Scott Gibson, courtesy *Fine Homebuilding*, © The Taunton Press, Inc. Drawings by Paul Perreault, © The Taunton Press, Inc.

p. 76: A Deliberate Neighborhood by John Abrams, issue 139. All photos by Kevin Ireton, courtesy Fine Homebuilding, © The Taunton Press, Inc., except photo p. 87 © Philippe Jordi. Drawings by Mark Hannon, © The Taunton Press, Inc.

p. 88: A House with Wings by Dan Rockhill, issue 139. All photos by Charles Bickford, courtesy *Fine Homebuilding,* © The Taunton Press, Inc., except photos p. 95 © Dan Rockhill. Drawings p. 94 (top) by Vince Babak and p. 94 (bottom) by Mark Hannon, © The Taunton Press, Inc.

p. 96: Modern Living in a New England Village by Scott Simons, issue 148. All photos © Brian Vanden Brink. Drawings p. 102 (top) by Dan Thornton and p. 102 (bottom) by Mark Hannon, © The Taunton Press, Inc.

p. 104: Red House by Paul and Peggy Duncker, issue 147. All photos by Charles Miller, courtesy Fine Homebuilding, © The Taunton Press, Inc., except photo p. 108 © Paul Duncker. Drawings by Mark Hannon, © The Taunton Press, Inc.

p. 112: Designing a Historical House by Kevin McKenna, issue 123. All photos by Andy Engel, courtesy *Fine Homebuilding,* © The Taunton Press, Inc. Drawings by Scott Bricher, © The Taunton Press, Inc.

p. 120: A California Home Designed with the Future in Mind, issue 131. Photos pp. 121, 123 © Bruce Kelley. Photo p. 122 by Charles Bickford, courtesy *Fine Homebuilding,* © The Taunton Press, Inc. Drawings by Scott Bricher, © The Taunton Press, Inc.

p. 126: Texas Saddlebag House by Todd Hamilton, issue 123. Photos pp. 126, 129, 131 by Roe A. Osborn, courtesy Fine Homebuilding, © The Taunton Press, Inc. Photos pp. 128, 132 (bottom) © Todd Hamilton. Photos pp. 130, 132 (top) © Craig Kuhner. Drawings by Scott Bricher, © The Taunton Press, Inc.

p. 134: Built Intending to Stay by Mark Primack, issue 124. All photos by Andy Engel, courtesy *Fine Homebuilding,* © The Taunton Press, Inc. Drawings © Mark Primack.

p. 142: Guest House by the Bay by Peter Zimmerman, issue 131. All photos by Tim O'Brien, courtesy *Fine Homebuilding,* © The Taunton Press, Inc. Drawings by Scott Bricher, © The Taunton Press, Inc.

p. 150: Round Roof in the City by Dan Parke, issue 146. All photos by Andy Engel, courtesy *Fine Homebuilding,* © The Taunton Press, Inc., except photos p. 157 © Sandy MacDonald. Drawings p. 155 by Rick Daskam and 156 by Ron Carboni, © The Taunton Press, Inc.

p. 158: Simple House, Contemporary Look by Rob Kovitz, issue 130. All photos by Charles Bickford, courtesy Fine Homebuilding, © The Taunton Press, Inc. Drawings by Dan Thornton, © The Taunton Press, Inc.

p. 166: A Cozy Vermont House by Leslie Hill, issue 124. All photos by Charles Bickford, courtesy *Fine Homebuilding,* © The Taunton Press, Inc. Drawings by Vince Babak, © The Taunton Press, Inc.

p. 174: Part Office, Mostly House by Kathryn Porter, issue 123. All photos by Charles Miller, courtesy *Fine Homebuilding,* © The Taunton Press, Inc. Drawings by Scott Bricher, © The Taunton Press, Inc.

The articles in this book originally appeared in *Fine Homebuilding* magazine. The date of first publication, issue number, and page numbers for each article are given at right.